Zero Second Thinking

Thinking

The world's simplest training

for improving your mind

Breakthrough Partners

Yuji Akaba

INTRODUCTION

People with wholehearted intention who in reality are at a standstill are surprisingly common.

No forward progress. Or, spinning your wheels. When there's something you're hung up on, your mind doesn't work well, and your thoughts just don't run deep. Even if you try to think, some other immediate task floats into your mind. You can't concentrate. You flit to and fro, end up running in circles, unable to reach a conclusion, incapable of getting to the core of it all.

Prior to thinking deeply, it is progress to be able to think even a little bit constructively. When you waver, fretting at the entrance to the challenge whether it's this or that, you won't progress even a single step forward, let alone be able to think deeply. You've thought about it, so much that you're tired of thinking, and even then you've made no headway.

From the start, the majority of people have no understanding of how to *think deeply*.

You're told to *please think harder*, told *this idea is shallow*, and you understand that others are demanding you to think deeply. When we're able to think deeply, we somehow feel that we're able to accomplish amazing things, but no one knows a concrete methodology for doing so. Even when we think we might have it, we lack confidence.

Taking a moment to think back, from elementary school onwards in Japan, thinking exercises which require us to effectively assemble our thoughts are mostly absent. Instruction on how to deepen our thinking is, aside from sparse composition exercises, also mostly absent. And of opportunities to speak in class, the majority are in response to the teacher's questions. Chances to battle out opinions like in America are also mostly absent. Which is to say nothing of the fact that manners of thinking, methods of coping with one's troubles, and so forth, are not covered at all.

I believe that those who can make ordinary conversation, read books, and use the internet are inherently intelligent. Some people are susceptible to stress and pressure, but everyone has their own opinions and can express them when in a comfortable environment. Everyone also possesses appropriate powers of judgment. To be certain, some ideas are shallow and some deep, but this too will improve through conversing with others. Age, academic record, sex, experience, and so on play little role in this. Even so, surprisingly many people have no confidence in themselves, and their precious potential becomes a squandered resource.

This is such a waste. With a method for organizing one's mind, for gathering and deepening one's thoughts, anyone can grow as though they are a different person. They will be able to excel at work. Their communication troubles will diminish, and they will be liberated in no small way from unnecessary suffering, capable of living freer than before.

I was involved in management innovation at McKinsey, a consulting firm, for fourteen years, and since the year 2000 have been engaged in cofounding startups and management support. Management innovation refers to attacking head-on the management challenges companies confront, improving profitability, implementing organizational reform, launching new enterprises, and developing human resources. I work with CEOs, executives, department heads, section managers, and other high-level leaders to promote awareness and behavioral reform. Since the fighting power of company employees greatly influences the future of companies, it is imperative that each employee grow to consider matters more deeply, devise solution strategies, and leave no stone unturned.

Concurrently, through various encounters, I've had frequent chances to speak and interact with many people, including opportunities to counsel students at business plan contests and venture-related university lectures.

Fortunately, through such efforts and connections with many people, I've worked out an effective method for deepening one's thoughts and organizing one's mind.

It doesn't matter whether you're an elementary school student or a university student or a working-adult, whether you're a man or a woman, or whether you have a good academic background or not. Nationality, too, matters not. No matter who you are, this method produces startling results.

It simply entails writing down, one after another, whatever floats into your mind. Write these not in a notebook or on a computer, but simply use one piece of Letter paper per thought.

Rather than leisurely spending time on each, quickly finish one page in within one minute. Write 10 pages every day then instantly organize them by throwing them into one of several folders. Just by doing this, you can train the most fundamental *ability to think*, something which is not adequately taught even in McKinsey's program. You will not only be able to think deeply, but will also approach the ultimate level of "Zero Second Thinking." You will become the master of your mind; stress and anxiety will fall away. You'll begin living with eyes on your own bright future. Moreover, it costs almost no money, and in just three weeks' time you can expect to feel considerable results.

From here on, I will introduce the concrete method. Chapters 1 and 2 further elucidate tips for thinking and what I mean by "Zero Second Thinking." Those who want to put note-taking into practice and draw nearer to "Zero Second Thinking" as soon as possible may begin reading from Chapter 3.

Contents

Chapter 2: Humans Can Think in Zero Seconds

Chapter 3: The Note-taking Method for Cultivating Zero Second Thinking

Contents

Chapter 4: Utilizing Notes to the Fullest Extent

- Jotting down ideas one after another

- Laying them out like a card game

- Adding and organizing new ideas as they come

- Balancing the whole

- Writing in PowerPoint while referencing notes

- Allowing your proposal several days to ripen then raising it to the next level with meticulous revisions

- Having them write notes for you

- Writing notes while listening to their worries

Chapter 5: Organizing and Utilizing Notes

Chapter 1

Tips for
"Thinking"

Putting into words the images and intuitions that come to your mind

To begin, I want for you to raise your awareness of the relationship between thoughts and words. Thoughts are formed by words, and emotions can be put into words. From there, let's try putting into words the images and intuitions that come to our minds.

It's common for our minds to feel foggy. Various words float around. Language that won't become words emerges and disappears. Let's try our best to put it into words. Let's try to put it into words the second it rises to the surface. Talk is cheap, however, and this language will continue to flicker without becoming distinct if left in the mind, so begin to write. Even if bad thoughts about this or that come to mind, write them without concern. "Without concern" means write people's names, or desirous or hateful or bitter things, exactly as they are. Find a way to work through unpleasant feelings and begin writing. Having done that, after expelling it all out, strangely enough, you will become able to be just a little more forward-looking.

Here's an example of what that might look like:

Why doesn't my boss let me do that project?

Is there something about me he's not satisfied with? Last time, too, he didn't pass on the project I raised my hand for.

Even though I definitely would have done a good job.

I wonder why he didn't have me do it.

Why does he never pass these on to me?

I wonder if they don't have high hopes for me in this division.

However, yesterday he praised me quite a bit. That was unusual. Maybe I'm appreciated more than I think.

Maybe there's a different reason for my not being given those projects.

Unless—maybe there's some different project he's considering me for?

I'm probably overthinking it. But still.

I guess fretting over it won't help anything.

Tomorrow, I'll try asking him directly!

Or it might look like this:

Why did that turn into an argument between me and him?

I guess it's because I wasn't very thrilled about his birthday present for me even though he went to all that trouble to buy it.
But it wasn't even really my taste.

Was there really any need to buy something like that?

Last time was something weird too.

But I guess he's really putting in the effort, not forgetting my birthday or our anniversary, especially considering how men can be.

And he does seem serious about me.

He did say he worked extra hard at his part-time job to

save up for it.

I think I might've stuck my foot in my mouth.

Maybe I'll try apologizing.

But it's not like I'm in the wrong. It's not even my taste.

However, he did go the extra mile at work to buy it for me, even though he's busy preparing for his test.

He might not look it, but he's pretty serious about school, so juggling both studying and work must've been difficult.

Hmmm…

His fashion sense *is* somewhat lacking.

But still…

I'll go ahead and send him an email saying sorry.

Ah, he replied. He must've been waiting for it. Good thing I sent it!

There may be times your mood doesn't change, no matter how much you write. Nevertheless, in most cases, when you set out to write without reservation, in the end your feelings will be a little clearer. As a result of writing out what you want to say without hesitation regardless of what others might think of your words, you will feel refreshed. This is the same as how shedding tens of thousands of tears after a horrible heartbreak allows you to begin moving forward again.

Although it might feel bewildering at first—wondering *can I really write down something like this?*—you will soon get used to it. You can keep them somewhere no one will see. Since there's no chance that others will see what you write, there's no need to worry.

Although you might feel ashamed, wonder if you can really write such things down, once you force yourself to try to write it out, you will realize that you're surprisingly capable. We have the expression "to spin a tale," but it really is just like that.

Not spinning a tale, but spinning together your own emotions. Because there's no need to hold back on anybody's behalf, you'll quickly lengthen it out. If you begin putting pen to paper from the moment an idea comes to mind, then this is something that even those who think themselves no good at writing can accomplish. Trying to write neatly ends in no writing at all, but you can write as much as you'd like as long as you don't worry about order and phrasing. There's nothing you can't write so long as you don't worry about the public eye. Especially with negative emotions, there are no bounds to what is okay to write.

Everyone, while awake, is always feeling something. They are thinking something; there is some kind of image in their mind. However, it quickly disappears. Prior to becoming cognizant of language, these murky feelings disappear without pointing to anything specific. We forget them briefly, but this does not mean the source of our uneasiness has resolved itself. Pent-up feelings do not disappear of their own accord. So, we feel more and more depressed.

Something's off, I don't feel good; I'm antsy but I can't put my finger on why; Something's wrong, but it can't be helped so I'll try to forget about it—everyone has experienced these feelings before. Or, rather, experiences them multiple times every single day. In that situation, it's normal to forget about these feelings, but there they pool in the bottom of one's heart, becoming heavy over time.

My recommendation is to put them into words, writing them down without reservation. To do so is to expel your pent-up feelings of unease from your body. It doesn't mean you will be showing them to anybody. There is absolutely no need for reservation. Just because you've acknowledged your feelings of unease in writing, it does not mean they will then manifest in reality, and it does not mean anything bad will happen.

Anger, dissatisfaction, anxiety, and the like are easier to recognize than general unease—easier to understand, and easier to put into words. As long as one does not hesitate to write these out, anyone can become capable of writing freely. It's a matter of getting used to writing.

There are likely many people who adhere to principles of not wanting to complain or badmouth others. Thinking this way is truly a praiseworthy thing. But in this state, nevertheless, rinsing oneself clean is not so easy. People who can digest these feelings, first of all, do not exist. Shutting one's eyes to these feelings, or forcibly trying to lock them away, will invariably end with them erupting back out. In cases when they don't hit that person themself, they will strike other people and ultimately come out the wrong way. If this is so, then it is better to put worries aside and let them spew out onto paper (of course, without showing others; lock them away somewhere they will definitely not be seen).

Also, in everyday life or at work, you may have constructive thoughts and ideas. But at the same time, certain feelings—that it's futile, that there's no way *you* could do it, that it's impossible—will also come welling up. Anxiety will surge forth. It is good to write all of this down as well. Write before you can give it a second thought. Without trying to clean it up, put it into words and write it out exactly as it comes.

Done in this way, the grand scheme of your constructive thoughts and ideas will rise into view before your very eyes. Things that bother you, things you think are good— it will all come gushing out. In times when you're hung up on something and can't think on to the next level, too, you will come to be alert. These are not business proposals you will show to your higher-ups, so without any undue concern, begin writing from the things that bother you, from the things you notice.

Aiming to use your words freely and precisely

As you grow used to putting images and intuitions into words, you will become increasingly able to express your feelings and thoughts without strain. What you want to say will quickly come out, so there will be no stress. You will be able to express yourself in writing without hesitating over things like word choice. As you continue on, you will become more and more capable of expressing yourself smoothly.

When you are able to express yourself smoothly, you can communicate with others easily, whether that be at work or in private matters. You will be understood quickly. You'll become able to relax when you write and speak, which will allow you to be your ordinary self, putting others at ease. Thereupon others will also relax, and their understanding will increase, too.

Communication is most effective when both parties are fully present and considerate of each other. This makes it easy to arrive at mutual understandings, and of course unlikely to turn into an argument.

Even in cases where your partner has a question, it will be a question which has arisen *after* you've explained your situation well, so the conversation will proceed smoothly. Having done this, your exchange will be enjoyable, and whatever explanation or discussion will move one step forward. Questions which miss the mark are unlikely to appear, so while mutually enjoying your conversation, you'll be able to continue feeling good about your questions and explanations.

When you are able to communicate in this way, you can be present at meetings in a natural manner, and so you will grow able to communicate more naturally than ever—*without* stifling your emotions or excessively posturing. This does not look like a screaming match or an emotional showdown. It looks like: *With respect to your question, I think I would like to proceed while thoroughly confirming the delivery date and cost such that both companies benefit.* Or, it looks like: *I think this might be slightly difficult in terms of cost and delivery date, so with regards to the additional function which was proposed a few days ago, I would be extremely grateful if you could postpone it until Phase 2.* In this way, you will grow capable of communicating politely yet straightforwardly.

Even in slightly more difficult situations, it looks like this: *About the discussion at last week's planning meeting—we had a misunderstanding and I was a bit distraught by it, but after discussing the special circumstances with my boss she was very understanding. From here on, I'll be sure to request your con-*

firmation in advance. Or, it might possibly look like: *With regards to being introduced to your engineer—because I've not received a reply after trying to get in touch several times, we have decided to move forward with someone else. Since for the time being we have found a promising candidate, there will no longer be any need for an introduction this time.* Such are examples of polite and straightforward communication. Respect the other party's viewpoint while not giving in to compromise or adopting a servile attitude.

In situations where you're worried about ruining the other party's good mood or causing an argument, when you are able to smoothly communicate things you thought you were absolutely incapable of expressing, these meetings will proceed constructively, which means needless discomfort will be hard-pressed to arise. There will be no strange restraint or adjusting your story to fit the situation, so you can feel good about it. Times when you are able to problem-solve before things get too complicated—from being overly self-conscious or overly hesitant—will increase, so your work will come to run smoothly. Towards complex and intricate problems, too, you will become able to retain control.

In many jobs, work proceeds through the piecemeal accumulation of conversational and email exchanges. Progress becomes easy if these are performed with accuracy and without undue restraint. If problems deteriorate from time to time, this is due to countermeasures delayed by excessive restraint and indecision—problems and discrepancies which could have been resolved early on but were neglected. As long as these problems are not neglected, appropriate, necessary action can be taken. Once you're able to use words freely and precisely, these will all end in your favor.

Even if you are polite, communicating without excessive restraint may not come easily at first. It is to be expected that you will most likely experience discomfort. Many people have their own experiences of past blunders, and they manage work while trying not to communicate what they're thinking. These people, in trying to avoid being told that they're *just oblivious*, have perhaps in fact become excessively heedful of their work atmosphere.

Even among friends, they've caused terrible problems by saying something the second they thought it. Or, they were thinking it would cause a problem. Therefore, it is likely the case that even when they have something they want to say, they swallow it and wash it down without really clarifying what it is. Without a doubt, saying things the second one thinks them without considering how the other party will take it does indeed frequently end in fights. However, in these cases, it is perhaps that prior to communicating these thoughts, the content of them was a tad one-sided and coming from a biased perspective. As a result, hesitancy towards speaking their minds grows stronger.

In this emotional state, we become incapable of expression itself. When we become incapable of expression, feelings of helplessness and of giving up come into being, and thought itself ceases to occur.

There will never be a time when you experience growth under conditions in which you do not need to think. If you do not think to organize matters and solve the problems at hand, your feelings, too, will never become clear. Your motivation will decline, work will lose its appeal, and results will become hard-pressed to materialize. If you are in a situation like this, you must release yourself from it at once.

As you accumulate experience putting images and intuitions into words, to this extent you'll become able to shape them without resistance. Hesitation towards putting them into words will fall away. Before you know it, you will be able to write. You will be able to write and speak with surprisingly little strain, and you will become able to communicate without harming the other party's mood.

Having come this far, you'll at last approach the stage

of, in the truest sense, having grown used to words and being able to use them. As naturally as eating dinner or watching TV, you'll be able to use words skillfully. Resistance and indecisiveness towards words will go away, and you'll become able to use them freely, precisely. From an overly-sensitive, overly-timid state of paralysis, you will embark on a huge move forward.

Grasping the central meaning and nuances of words

In verbalizing thoughts and in communication also, caution is necessary regarding nuances in the meaning of words.

In each word, there is a central meaning. Within a given region, era, community or circle of friends, there is a meaning which everyone can more or less imagine or comprehend. When we say "morning," we generally indicate the period before noon. Most Japanese people will comprehend that it means the time up until noon. Depending on the industry there may be people who consider until 2 PM to be morning, but they are not a large crowd. As to the question of what time morning ends, there is not much deviation.

However, depending on the person, there is a wide range of opinion as to what time morning starts. People who set out at 3 AM and work in the morning are not few. On the other hand, there are certainly also those who think morning begins at 6 AM, and there are also those who sleep until 9:30 AM and so think morning begins from then.

Words used to express "school," "work," "bicycle," and other things/objects often possess a relatively commonly shared meaning. Among the objects present in reality which these words indicate, there are old ones and new ones, but to that extent there is very little room for misunderstanding or discrepancy. This is because adding qualifiers is sufficient: "that new bicycle" or "the bicycle in the storage room which I rode when I was in elementary school," etc. The meaning is decidedly unambiguous.

Similarly, expressions used to convey emotion, such as "painful," "sad," and "I love you," seem vague, but they hold a relatively similar meaning for the majority of people. It's not to the same degree as things/objects, but they signify relatively close concepts.

On the other hand, in the case of phrases like "give it your all," "sense of responsibility," and "I will do this without fail," the meaning differs considerably between people. There is considerable deviation based on each person's standards, values, background, history of success, history of failure, and so on. Everyone determines a word's meaning based on their own criteria, and we exchange words without being very aware of this.

If there are those for whom "giving it your all" indicates putting in the effort from 10 AM to 6 PM, then there are also those who take this phrase to mean working over 18 hours in a single day. If there are those for whom staying up all night is a matter of course, then there are also those for whom such things are out of the question. Among those for whom staying up all night is out of the question, there are those whose reasoning lies in not understanding the meaning of trying so hard, and there are also those whose reasoning is that because their efficiency the following day would suffer, they will absolutely not stay up all night—*even if* they are giving it their all.

As for a "sense of responsibility," depending on the person, one might be at the level of understanding this as the sentiment of needing to carry out something using all available means, even staking one's honor and life on its successful completion. Meanwhile, someone else might be at the level of thinking well, because there's something they have to do, may as well go ahead and do what's within their capabilities. In more severe cases, it's well within the realm of possibility that there are those who actively try to not consider the meaning of words.

In this way, for all words, within a given region, era, or community, there is a central meaning which the majority collectively understands, and there are wider degrees of amplitude that belong to individuals or subcommunities.

Even within the same word, there are cases where the central meaning has different shades of nuance. It is possible that white signifies not white, but grey—or, in extreme cases, even black.

In light of this, it becomes necessary to always consider and more deeply understand precisely what your words and the words of others signify, whether a remark has intentions behind it, and whether something is said consciously or unconsciously.

Moreover, it is exceedingly useful at both work and in one's private life to always consider and more deeply understand the range of meanings in each word, the ways in which meaning can veer from a word's most common usage, and how interpretations of nuance can vary from person to person. But this is not merely useful. At times, it is of decisive importance.

As a consequence of such fluctuations in meaning, the speech of those who possess a keen intuition towards language and utilize precise wording appropriate to each situation is extremely easy to understand.

Their words do not blur. You can comprehend exactly what they are trying to say. There's never a worry as to what they are trying to say, as to what meaning they are using. There's never a misunderstanding. Communication is conducted effectively.

If there are any people in your life who speak in an easily understandable way, I want for you to make a point of noticing their lingual intuition, their word choice, and so on. One by one, their words will enter directly into your mind. You will notice how artlessly they speak intelligibly, how their word choice is precise, clear. Not only are their explanations easy to understand, but also it is difficult to feel uncomfortable about the content of their conversation. Even when they are explaining a new concept, you nod your head and indeed understand well. The meaning of each word is precise, their usage is in line with our comprehension of it, and if it is different then they explain how so. Nothing is forced, and there are no sudden leaps during the conversation.

With people like this, not only is their wording clear, but also their stance and talking points, so they frequently perform well at work. They themselves are never confused, they never cause confusion among those they work with, and everything proceeds in an orderly fashion.

Their words are unambiguous and moreover straight-forward, so it is easy to for them to leave favorable impressions. They never couch things in inappropriate terms, and they never needlessly dampen others' enthusiasm. Deservedly, they are popular and make outstanding leaders.

Because they are always conceptually sharp, and moreover can say what they want to say without strain, they don't really get stressed out. They can easily communicate their intentions and emotions. When we aren't stressed, we can communicate in a relaxed manner, and doing so helps the listener relax as well, which makes us easy to comprehend. This becomes a wellspring of leadership.

It is common that when someone is intelligent and capable of work, in fact their lingual intuition is sharp, which renders their communicative abilities visible and allows them to shine.

Well then, what about those whose intuition with language is dull? With such people, not only is their wording complex and difficult to understand, but also their thinking itself tends to be vague and ambiguous. Even if they're the one talking, little by little they veer off track, get flustered and continue on about meaningless things. Without someone to stop them, there are even people who will continue talking like this for twenty or thirty minutes.

Avoiding shallow thinking and wheel spinning

People who believe themselves to have keen lingual intuition, and beyond that to think competently, are perhaps common.

Well then, no matter the circumstances, to promptly grasp the state of affairs, to think *because this is this way it will turn out like this, and the reason for that is this*, or to think *the emergency countermeasures for this should be this, and further on we can expect to have to do this*—people who can assemble their thoughts in this way and explain them are quite few and far between.

For example, in the case of a speech to raise one's team's productivity:

"In order to raise our team's productivity, I'd like to move forward with curtailing meeting time. Speaking of meetings, you'll be in trouble if you don't properly clean up the meeting room after using it. How many times per week on average do you all attend meetings?

Right now, they take roughly an hour and a half to two hours, don't they? The same people speak every time. And those who don't speak don't speak at all, isn't that right? In any case, everyone make sure to be present, and let's increase our productivity."

It's hard to tell what's going on. What does "productivity" mean? This person is not thinking deeply about how to tie up his remarks. Hence why he proposes to raise team productivity and then, as far as actions go, ends on the off-topic remark of "make sure to be present."

While of course he probably understands the meanings of his words, he's not in the habit of thinking very deeply about them, so the result is overly emotional. He's not accurately grasping the meaning of each individual word, and without noticing where his topic has shifted, he is unable to skillfully continue until his conclusion. Those listening of course cannot follow along, so progress at work is slow.

With people like this, not only are their talking points ambiguous and confusing to those listening, but also they end up trying to say one thing then go too far and inadvertently hurt others, and then they try to gloss over the situation with a stale joke which has the adverse effect of killing everyone's mood, and they are liable to one way or another cause problems when dealing with others. There are likely several people in your life who strike you as fitting this description. Or alternatively, perhaps *you* are that person.

Meanwhile, here's what the speech of someone who stays on topic looks like:

"In order to raise our team's productivity, I'd like to move forward with curtailing meeting time. At present, meetings which last upwards of an hour and a half make up more than half of all meetings. If things don't go well, meetings which last two hours or longer are also quite likely. If we think about why these meetings are long, several primary reasons come to mind.

Number one is that the purpose of meetings is unclear, causing talks to drag on.

Number two is that, as a result of number one, discussion veers far off track.

Number three is that each person's contributions are long yet have unclear conclusions.

Number four is that no one considers the cost of meetings, and instead everyone simply thinks it good to gather and talk.

These are among other reasons. So, I think I'd like for us to brainstorm countermeasures for each.

This goes back to issue number one, but because the purpose for holding meetings is as unclear as it is, and because those who participate don't have a good grasp of what should be accomplished, it is common to see meetings drag on in idle conversation. As for this, from now on, when convening a meeting, I'd like for us to clarify three things: the purpose for holding the meeting, the topics to be discussed, and the expected end time. Next time, I'd like to review how much improvement has been made with respect to these changes. Now, as for issue number two…"

If one can speak in this way, they will be easy to understand and never drift away from the matter at hand. They will naturally demonstrate leadership, and problem-solving will proceed swimmingly. Their experiences of success will increase, and what's more, they will turn into an outstanding leader.

As seen above, even if the average person considers themself to think well, in reality they frequently engage in "shallow thinking" and "wheel spinning." This is not so much a matter of being smart or dull, but rather due to a lack of training.

"Shallow thinking," as the name suggests, is the condition of not thinking deeply, of only ever thinking on a surface-level. Due to this lack of thinking, such people quickly find themselves at a loss when asked the meaning of something they've said. Their defense is full of holes, as they are not thinking about the meaning of the words they use, or how the other party might interpret them, or how best to explain them. In situations like this, prior to becoming hard-pressed for an explanation, the thinking itself is often mistaken in the first place.

"Wheel spinning" refers to thinking on a single issue deeply, ultimately only stroking the surface without implementing any higher-quality problem-solving. Within the debate of how to curtail meeting time, one would not lapse into spinning their wheels if they were to deeply think upon why meetings are long, which parts of them are long, what the bottleneck preventing meetings from being shortened is, and have others ask questions about how they can be shortened. Sooner or later, they would be able to draw near to the heart of the matter.

Even so, many people still hesitate to ask questions. It would appear that in Japan there is still a culture and atmosphere of thinking it rude to ask questions. In Europe and America, far livelier Q&A sessions are held, which is probably why exchange students find themselves perplexed at first. What's more, there's also the worse problem which precedes hesitating to ask questions—namely that of questions not coming to mind due to a low awareness of the issues at hand.

When thinking or discussion gets caught in wheel spinning, no matter how much time is spent, one's thinking will not move forward. It will not deepen. Consequently, it ends with superficial, conventional ideas.

Why does this happen? Unfortunately, it is because in Japan, from elementary school through college, exercises in thinking deeply, exercises in truly thinking seriously— they were scantily carried out.

I mentioned this shortcoming of formal education at the beginning of this book, but in fact, even across fourteen years of training at McKinsey, despite having had task organization, analysis, and strategy planning thoroughly drilled into me, I was mostly not instructed in the methodology for thinking quicker and deeper, or in the methodology for making my mind function at the highest possible speed while still maintaining internal quietude and sorting out my feelings. I suppose the premise was that things thought to be exceedingly fundamental would, as a matter of course, already be incorporated into everyone's personal skill set. Nevertheless, no matter how you slice it, there are huge differences from person to person, and I definitely think there were few people who were maintaining internal quietude and sorting out their feelings.

Steadily deepening your thinking, presenting all of the options then evaluating and arranging them in order of priority—the truth is that things like this are the same as weight training in that the more you train, the more powerful you become. For those who have finished reading this book and begun ten-pages-a-day note-taking, in a few weeks' time, I can have you personally feeling effects like those of weight training.

As a result of this training, your mental organizational skills will soar, and you will grow able to use precise language. With training, anyone can do it. Academic background, work history, experience, and position have absolutely nothing to do with it. And of course, factors like gender, nationality, and age also play no role. Despite the fact that it's something that can be strengthened in this way, the majority of people are spinning their wheels without knowing it.

There are also, of course, geniuses of thinking who have no connection to such efforts. Professional shogi players fit this mold of non-verbal thinking. Professional shogi players read over a hundred moves ahead and still remember this many years later. However, thinking which relies on language is different. To be able to think properly, and to communicate using appropriate language absolutely does not require brains like theirs. All of us can, in accordance with training, think magnitudes deeper, understand the meaning of words exactly right, and acquire a command of language.

Both "deep meditation" and "just talking" are difficult

Let's look at it from a slightly different angle. We have the term "deep meditation," but just by intently turning our thoughts over, considering whether something is this or that, our thinking is unlikely to progress. In most cases, it becomes a waste of time.

It would be nice if we could deepen our thoughts through meditation, but for most people, trivial ideas or anxieties arise then disappear, arise then disappear, for the most part never taking shape. Because we don't record them in writing they don't accumulate, and our ideas also fail to deepen.

Unrelieved, we search for some related story on the internet, and without really finding any good ideas, one or two anxious hours pass before we even realize it. We think we have a good idea, then when we look it up we think otherwise. When we search again, we think another idea might be better, then when we look into it more the drawbacks become apparent.

We're distressed by ourselves and our thoughts ultimately become unmanageable, and after going in circles exhausting ourselves, we're back at square one.

On the other hand, there are those who talk to someone else the moment something comes to mind. No matter what it is, they say everything. It's often that in the process of talking, they themselves come to see various things and generate new ideas.

As it is, this is a fine method; however, in talking it out, upon getting a reaction of some degree, in most cases you will more quickly see results if you, rather than continuing to talk, change gears and record your thoughts up until that point in writing, further deepening your hypothesis. By writing, you'll temporarily organize your thoughts—after that, try resuming speaking. This structure facilitates swift PDCA (Plan, Do, Check, Act).

Although keeping your composure might still make this okay, one thing to be careful about when speaking to others is letting your emotions lead the way. While venting your emotions and speaking discursively might be more refreshing (you might even thank your partner for listening and feel more motivated), this will be unbearable for your listener. No matter how close your relationship is, they will slowly come to keep you at arm's length. More than anything, you will never master the essential skill of thinking for yourself, organizing the issues at hand, and making clear the best way to proceed.

Therefore, what I recommend is to record all of your thoughts in writing. When you write down each step of your thinking and whatever comes to your mind, instances in which you find yourself going in circles will almost wholly disappear. You will cease to simply vent your emotions. When you have what you've written in front of your eyes, you will naturally proceed with the next step forward. Your thinking will progress without strain. *Anyone* can do it.

What can I do to shorten meetings? For people who consider this question earnestly yet tend to think in circles, by writing down their thoughts, it becomes possible to sort the present situation, analyze why meetings run long, put forward several methods for shortening them, and list out concrete actions that can be taken.

In the event of writing down your thoughts, choosing wording too deliberately will halt your thinking. Alternatively, it is far and away better to write words out one after another without considering too deeply. Those who think *if I could just do that I wouldn't have any hardship*, or those who are aware of their weak points—it would seem that there are many people like this, but in fact this is not hard to do. If you set your heart on doing it, it will come relatively quickly. It's a simple matter of practice. By the time you finish this book, you will *without exception* to some degree acquire the aforementioned capabilities. Your mind will set to work as much as you'd like. I'd like for you to have faith in this as you continue reading.

To a certain extent, after relinquishing your concerns to paper, you will feel lighter, ideas will occur to you at a surprising rate, and your thinking will deepen. The big picture which you previously couldn't see will steadily unfold before you.

The big picture becoming easier to see is, put another way, understanding what the heart of the matter is, understanding what direction you are headed, and being able to organize the overall composition of it all. Put in terms of materials, this would mean being able to make a table of contents.

You say something, then say something else, consider what's next, synthesize it at the end, and in this way you can systematize your thinking. If you do this, you'll be able to better organize your mind, ideas will spring up more often, and oversights in your thinking process will decrease. And even to those who listen to your explanations, you will become exceedingly easy to understand.

There are probably many people who have, when writing business proposals, propositions, reports and the like, had the experience of ideas coming out in rapid succession after somehow solidifying a table of contents despite grumbling along in the beginning. It is possible to devise these quicker and more intentionally.

Chapter 2

Humans Can Think in Zero Seconds

Taking time does not necessarily lead to deeper thinking

There are sometimes people who prefer, with an important task, to spend all the PM hours on it or discuss it until morning. This way of thinking seeks to exhaust the argument. Depending on the company, this can be the norm. This is not uncommon even at small start-ups, which need to use their time properly to a greater extent than large companies.

Even so, it is quite dubious as to whether meetings like this are productive, whether participants are able to pin down the important points, whether they are able to accurately grasp the situation and make decisions, or whether action soon follows. One of course has the feeling of having worked. When one argues exhaustively, one has the feeling of having passed a productive day. However, whether this company can exercise decision-making at the necessary speed is extremely doubtful.

From the start, spending all the PM hours or continuing from evening until midnight, or if things don't go well continuing until daybreak—even just calculated among those present at the meeting, such practices cost a colossal amount.

Moreover, since it squanders stamina and willpower,

recovery costs a proportional amount of time. Beyond this, the reality is that during meetings, subordinates who don't participate in the discussion end up waiting around in vain. Even when higher-ups think their subordinates naturally must be doing their work, the more important a meeting is, the more difficult it is to continue with one's work until the outcome is clear.

To make matters worse, when management is away for long periods of time on retreats or vision meetings, while the bosses are out, subordinates tend to wait around aimlessly without accomplishing much work. The more higher-ups nag and fail to delegate authority well, the more they create this kind of situation.

In this regard, fear creeps in as to how many days it will cost for the entire organization to return to cruising speed. Just in returning to cruising speed, the aggregate loss of hundreds of hours cannot be recovered. I cannot think that the wastefulness deployed in the service of management achieving a feeling of a productivity can be justified. The content of crucial discussions becomes exceedingly sloppy proportional to the amount of time spent—no, *as a result of the time spent*. Expending time might lift your spirits, but content is a different matter. Taking time does not necessarily lead to deeper thinking.

One's own work is the same way. Especially with the majority of desk work, time is wasted worrying and going around in circles.

Should I do this? Or should I do that? If I say it like this, what will my boss say? —these worries are inexhaustible. Even if it's decided that you will write up the proposal for the client meeting in two weeks, you wonder about what to do. Even if you make a decision, you decide to tweak it again. You encounter unexpected difficulties in your outline or overall composition. Even if you're able to scrape together a draft proposal after a few days, no matter what it doesn't fit the bill and you end up revising it over and over and over again. You still have a vivid memory of your boss screaming at you last time, so you can't readily consult with them either. Meanwhile, you begin worrying about whether the title is also a bit off or not. *Ahh, I only have two days left. I'll have to stay up all night again…* —you've probably had experiences like this.

Those who haven't are truly remarkable, but in my own experience, most people more or less fumble about their work worrying, moving along while carrying their feelings of unease. This is not really something with which your boss or seniors will help you. They will tell you what's wrong, but in the first place they probably won't be the ones to teach you how to think properly, what you can do to think better, or how to plan. Accordingly, you can't expect the quality of your output to take any drastic upturn either.

This is not just a great loss for your company—it's a great loss for you, too. Just cruising along is *not* something to aspire to. With this manner of working you will not undergo satisfactory growth. If you do not grow, your life will be boring in the truest sense of the word.

If the only problems were not growing or being bored, then working idly might be fine, but lately the risk of losing one's job for doing so is quickly rising. Lifetime employment is rare, even at big companies. Even if you're happy to have not been targeted during the downsizing this time, the next time is not so certain, and there's also the chance the company itself will go out of business. At that time, if you're still practicing a leisurely work ethic, your chances for reemployment will also drastically shrink.

Competent people and excellent managers make swift decisions

In this way, there are many people who think at a leisurely pace; however, there is a very small portion of outstanding people who produce great results while moving at a high speed. They don't waste a single minute. They gather information at an astounding speed, make decisions, and move from one action item to the next lightning-fast. They are capable, too, of polishing off a considerable volume of proposals at a surprising pace. Furthermore, the more time they spend, the better the content they produce.

However, people like this really make up a tiny fraction of the population. Most people endlessly expend time. Moreover, whether they rush or not, their thinking doesn't deepen. It is first of all not the case that spending twice as much time on something will produce twice as good of results.

What gives rise to such a disparity?

One factor is the lack of thinking exercises mentioned in the previous chapter. Exercises in how to increase efficiency, quickly assemble one's thoughts, analyze, delve deep, clearly organize and polish off tasks, set others to work and instantly attain results—exercises in these areas are mostly absent in schools and companies.

With new employees, it is common that they receive instruction in how to write documents and proper etiquette. However, for the most part they do not receive training in how to instantly take in information, how to sort out problems, how to think of solution strategies, or even in the fundamental work of *thinking* itself.

At McKinsey where I worked, those who were competent workers had good intuition to begin with, but in addition to this, techniques of the craft are inherited in the form of instruction from their seniors. When someone is thought to be incompetent and does not receive instruction in technique, they are branded as being *an average joe* or *an incompetent*. If one has a certain set of attributes and is able to show them off, they might by a stroke of luck be thrown in with the "competent" group, but for those for whom this is not the case, recovery from branding is difficult. This is not to say that there aren't those who with a mixture of effort and scheming are capable of growth; however, the start of the race is of considerable importance.

Another factor is a lack of the concept of productivity.

Every company grapples with raising productivity at their actual sites of manufacturing, but towards desk work such as email exchange and the generation of written proposals and reports, the concept of productivity is not very widespread, and systematic efforts are also rarely carried out.

When work is running excessively far behind, one is likely to be briskly reprimanded, but there is a tacit understanding that there should naturally be a variation in time taken depending on the person and subject matter. Manufacturing costs are managed in units of one cent or less, but how fast one is thinking, how quickly one is making decisions, how tremendously is their mind functioning—these aspects are not regarded as being all that important.

On the contrary, there's even the belief that by expending time, good ideas might be born in the time spent waiting, or that ideas will descend down from heaven. Accidental "divine revelations" are of course possible, but these belong to those who have put in a staggering effort, who have thought through to the limit and hit a wall, then one day catch a glimpse of the blue sky on the other side of that wall. Such revelations descend only for truly hardworking people, so when those putting in only an average amount of effort reference them, it's merely an excuse.

They want to produce results relative to the amount of

time spent, and this is wanted of them, but unfortunately for most people, the amount of time spent and their output/results are not proportional. The fast people are startlingly fast, and it's difficult to forgive how slow the slow ones are.

On the other hand, when we look at managers, most of them (especially the outstanding ones) make swift decisions. Of course, in times when it is necessary to deliberate cautiously, or when there are many consultees or interested parties, they move forward with procedures cautiously, but feeling-wise they make quick decisions. Even if they've agonized, they have the merits and demerits for proposal A, proposal B, and proposal C clearly in mind.

Why are outstanding managers and leaders able to make swift decisions?

It's because they habitually continue to think on this matter. They are not negligent in gathering necessary information. Antennas perked up, they are always highly attuned to their surroundings. They have abundant connections with specialists in each field. They have a plethora of advisors they can trust. They are constantly considering the very best scenario and the very worst scenario. Where they can apply pressure for a given outcome, movements of the competition—it's all on their mind. They are always prepping for battle, so nothing takes them by surprise. They're thoroughly capable of thinking on their feet accurately while still exercising caution.

Put a different way, towards everything, they are always creating hypotheses. Or, they will quickly be able to create one. After they've created a hypothesis, they scrutinize it. If a hypothesis falls apart upon scrutiny, they quickly reformulate it. This is done astonishingly fast but does not wander off course. For example, concerning a fortune-telling smartphone app targeted at women, this might look like:

For urban, female users in their late twenties, among whom rates of iPhone ownership are high, the time they would most likely enjoy fortune-telling content would be during downtime after returning home from 9 PM onwards. Therefore, in order to raise the active-user rate, how about releasing a limited-time promotion for fortune-telling content aimed at that time frame?

In scrutinizing this hypothesis, they would consider the following:

1. They would confirm through internet searches and the like whether or not the rate of iPhone ownership

is actually high or not among urban women in their late twenties. They would promptly phone up an expert in the field, and they would hear directly the frank feedback of many female users in their late twenties. Through this process, they would grasp such things as the awareness, values, and behavior of the target users, and they would acquire a sense of the playing field.

2. They would confirm through internet searches and hearing from experts whether targeting urban female users in their late twenties is even worthwhile or not, and whether this demographic's user-rates are actually high or not.

3. They would confirm through user interviews and such whether the target demographic actually does most frequently enjoy fortune-telling content after 9 PM. And in addition to hearing from users, they would also look into the findings of market research online to learn when target users are on their iPhones.

4. They would confirm with a friend who's an app director what kind of promotion target users would likely

respond to, and they would analyze the service data of their own company.

Through such considerations, they inspect their hypotheses. It's common for imagination and reality to have been different, so they quickly amend their hypotheses.

I said that this is common among those at the management level, but of course among contract employees and part-time workers, too, those who are competent really *are* competent. This is because humans are intrinsically intelligent beings.

The ultimate result: Zero Second Thinking

Once you are able to put your vague feelings into words on the spot and deepen your thoughts, not only will your thinking move more smoothly, but also its speed will increase too. What once took you three or four days to come up with will take but a few hours. A project which took you a month will, depending on what it is, become completable in a week's time. Your productivity will double, triple, quadruple, increase tenfold.

Your tasks will become organized, you will be able to see to the core of each problem, the natural solution strategy and its attendant options will come to mind, and you will understand the merits and demerits of each option. You will grow able to drive home countermeasures which pin down the essential nature and big-picture backdrop of each problem.

Thinking which has simultaneously achieved such quality and speed has arrived at "Zero Second Thinking."

Zero Second—in other words, being able to instantaneously recognize the situation, instantaneously organize its challenges, instantaneously think of a solution strategy, and instantaneously make decisions about what has to be done. Time to waver becomes zero; time to fret becomes zero.

Times when this can literally be done instantly are frequent, but there are also cases which take a little bit more time. Even in these cases, compared to up until then, there is a surprising increase in speed. You will become able to assess in the space of an instant what is happening in front of you, what type of phenomenon it is, then in the next instant think of several possible paths with which to proceed, compare the advantages and disadvantages of each, then on the spot determine which course to take.

It is reasonable to say that those who are habitually ruminating on planning and business operations are able to promptly deal with any abrupt changes because they have mastered "Zero Second Thinking." They're naturally able to read ahead. Even when it's not entirely clear, they are able to instantaneously view the general direction forward. They are the exact opposite of those who circuitously gather information and procrastinate on drawing a conclusion then let their anxiety get the best of them and move about confusedly berating their subordinates.

It's exactly like the story of Newton's epiphany upon seeing the falling apple (whether or not this anecdote is true is another matter). Towards a challenge that one has been habitually pondering, a flash of insight is born.

Ichiro Suzuki of the MLB is famous not only for batting but also for his splendid defense. The instant the batter hits the ball, you can bet he's deciding which direction to dart based on all the information—the course of the pitch, the sound and direction of the ball, the direction and speed of the wind.

If he were to spend half a second thinking, he wouldn't be able to make a diving catch for a line drive sailing a hair's width above the ground.

Since ancient times, humans have, when faced with a lion on the savanna, been deciding in the space of an instant whether to use their spear to fight, flee as fast as possible, or call for backup. There was no time to waver.

The lion before their eyes had its fangs bared and could have attacked at any moment. Faced with situations of eat or be eaten, we have considered all possible actions, compared their advantages and disadvantages, instantaneously decided, taken action, and survived. We surely never sat indecisively, agonizing over this or that. If we were creatures of indecision, we would have gone extinct long ago.

What I want to say is that humans have an inherent, magnificent capacity to make judgements and think—along with an ability to take action derived from these—but we live in a pampering environment where everything will work itself out even if we idle about, in an antiquated society that's liable to hammer down the nail that sticks out, with behavior aimed at not causing friction with our surroundings, under seniors who have warned us to think cautiously, through education systems rooted in rote learning, or under the discipline of conservative parents who demand good manners of us, and the final composite effect of this is to seal a lid over our precious abilities and send us back to a retrograde state.

Especially within Japan's formal education, memorization and trifling test-taking skills are emphasized.

Test scores are not determined based on the quality of one's mind or by a strengthening of our intrinsic ability to think and make decisions, but rather by the extent to which one has mastered particular techniques which pass only in the confined space of an exam. This looks like rote memorization of mathematical formulas and theorems, beginning tests from questions which look answerable, calculating backwards from probable looking answers, intensively practicing questions which are likely to appear that year based on trends from previous years, and so on.

It is likely a majority of people, by means of the excessively self-conscious dichotomies cultivated therein—of being competent or incompetent, a winner or a loser, smart or dumb, praised or not praised—who are bound hand and foot and unable to maximize their innate abilities.

If that's so, then if one is able to demolish their insecurities and unravel the bindings tied around their mind, it should be possible to exhibit the innate high capabilities which we all possess. There must be something one can do about this wasteful state of affairs. It's hardly possible that there's nothing that can be done. Believing this, I thought and thought and devised the "note-taking" which I explain later on.

Zero Second Thinking
and gathering information

Although I say "Zero Second Thinking," if one has a shortage of information, then of course a minimum amount of investigation and information gathering is necessary. Without doing so, you will have no base or framework from which to think and simply be shooting in the dark. With problems and solution strategies, if you don't have a certain level of background knowledge, your decisions will be too personally influenced and, depending on the situation, you might make serious misjudgments.

Getting in the habit of keeping your antenna perked up, of being highly attuned to and interested in various things, is important, but in time when even this is insufficient, the outcome will be further research, asking experts, and so on.

Once you grow used to this, you will develop a level of discernment in two aspects. The first is in regards to whether or not you have the information necessary to make appropriate decisions. You will grow to discern whether you should go right or left, what the necessary information is to make a decision between Plan A, Plan B, and Plan C, whether you possess this information or not, and what decision should be made depending on what direction the information points.

Say there are five varieties of necessary information or knowledge, then you will also grow to discern whether there are mutual links between them, and if there are, which kind of link is OK and which kind is not OK.

The second aspect is in regards to discerning from where and how best to acquire key information. Once you develop a highly critical mind, you will grow able to get an idea of what you know, what you don't know, where to look and who to ask for the necessary information you don't know, and how best to still be resourceful even when you don't gather new information.

The problem is that the majority of people spend too much time researching. They search the internet, attend industry events, read books, participate in drawn-out inconclusive debates, and on top of this go so far as to revisit the past log of online discussion groups, reading every line, altogether spending weeks on end researching. Such activity in itself is of course fine, but such people are liable to prolong making judgement calls and decisions.

If such prolongment were to improve the accuracy of policy decisions, then this would be fine, but most often that is not the case.

This is because actions are rarely taken to quickly formulate a hypothesis (*since it's this kind of problem perhaps this should be done right away*), verify it with the findings of gathered information, and then improve the accuracy of the hypothesis. Instead, it is more common to focus single-mindedly on gathering information, thus delaying a judgement and widening the wound, rendering one unable to carry out effective countermeasures.

When I say this, I occasionally get the following response:

In making swift decisions, I don't know how much research is too much. I'm always puzzled. And I'm always getting grilled by my higher-ups about whether or not I researched properly. I have no idea how long I should spend on it. The more I research, the more anxious I become.

At those times, I respond as such:

Please come up with three possible solutions for a challenge you might presently be facing. Write out three merits and demerits for each, and then begin gathering information after *you have a general idea of each. If you do so, you will be able to proceed swiftly in an action-oriented direction.*

Or, more often, I'll say: *Even if you don't gather new information, you are definitely capable of inferring to a certain extent what needs to be done.* In response, I am told: *Yes, you are right. One way or another I think I know which direction to move in.* This exchange is more common. When they don't accept this challenge, they start by trying to gather information. They try to put off making decisions. It's perhaps even that they research endlessly *in order to* put off making a tough decision.

As far as I know, those who have accumulated experience in a given workplace have, faint or not, some image of what must be done towards a given problem. However, because they are not sufficiently practiced in how to concretize this image, they do not know what to do and as such are convinced that that they need to begin by gathering information; or, they are fearful of rebukes or snide remarks from their bosses, so they simply adopt the safety strategy of continuing with information gathering. Especially within large companies, the staff organization is strong, endless pressure comes from every direction, and fault-finding is commonplace, so workers are apt to gather information excessively.

Should you go right, or should you go left? In order to decide this, what do you need to know? In reality, getting in the habit of keeping your antenna perked up to such matters is not such a difficult thing to do. This is because normal people, in other words the vast majority of people, have more or less functioning powers of discernment. What is holding you back from success is past traumatic experiences, rebukes from higher-ups, dwindling efficiency due to hierarchical organization, style guidelines from the bureaucracy, alienation from business, and so forth.

Of course, there is a trick necessary in creating a hypothesis then producing a policy with only the information you currently possess. It is also necessary to be strict with oneself. The trick is to keep a check on perfectionistic feelings of wanting more information while developing a knack for producing daring hypotheses. Just by doing so, the speed and quality of your hypothesis formulation will dramatically rise.

It seems difficult, but from the sense of achievement and progress gained by swiftly dealing with things you need to get done, your stress will instead be reduced.

The temptation of procrastination is there for anyone, but accelerating forward without mistakes is much better in the long run. If you are able to cope quickly, you will be able to do so before it's too late. Starting sooner also makes it easier to improve. The key lies in believing this to be better than emphasizing information gathering only to produce overdue results.

What one needs to be cautious of is that there are

some people who will, despite having a lack of information, not research at all, not consult with experts, not perk up their antenna, and work recklessly—all in the name of speed. Having tunnel vision and making decisions based on limited information, one's own preferences, or past rules of thumb while ignoring the fundamental actions of promptly gathering information, considering the big picture, devising alternatives, weighing your options, and firmly implementing your decisions thereafter—this is extremely dangerous. Leaving hypotheses at just that without seeking verification. It's a question of to which degree to do so, but it is necessary to review and verify at least the cores of your hypothesis.

Mastering Zero Second Thinking through note-taking

The quickest and best method for mastering Zero Second Thinking—which I've alluded to several times up until now—is "note-taking."

"Note-taking" was born from the process of, when I first entered McKinsey, receiving a large amount of helpful advice from my seniors about how to interview, how to analyze, team management, and so forth. Without omitting anything, I attempted to write it all down, and in doing so attempted to firmly grasp and make it my own.

However, across writing several thousand pages and also having many others write them as well, I realized that writing notes allows one to clear away self-consciousness and think about things honestly. I believe that the key was to, within the constraint of one minute, swiftly and without hesitation produce a substantial amount of writing.

"Note-taking" is a form of calisthenics for loosening a stiff intellect, an easy method for disciplining one's mind.

By recording in writing doubts and ideas the second they occur to you, your mind will steadily come to function better, and your emotions will become straightened out as well. The hardships of being imprisoned in self-consciousness will go away. By means of "note-taking," anyone can very quickly arrive at this mental state. Even you will be surprised at how quick your thinking becomes.

Concretely speaking, on horizontal sheets of Letter paper, using one page each time, with four to six lines per page and lines approximately ten to twenty words long, write ten pages per day, each within one minute. Accordingly, you will spend just ten minutes on note-taking each day. Refer to "Note 1" for an example (in this book, "one line" refers to all the contents following a single dash, regardless of whether the contents of a single dash spill over to the next line).

You might be wondering if such a straightforward method works, but the fact that it can be done easily and readily is the whole point.

Note 1 was written by the leader of sales of a major retail company who is in charge of roughly one thousand employees at a regional headquarters office. This person exhibits extraordinary excellence and normally responds to questions wonderfully as well, but he quickly resorts to shouting at his subordinates.

He confides in me that by shouting, his subordinates shrink back and nothing good comes of it, but that he still ends up doing so anyway against his better judgement.

He began by thinking of the title "If it were me, what kind of leadership would I want?" and then wrote six lines. The content is quite straightforward.

- I'd want them to make my tasks clear
- I'd want them to provide guidance on concrete actions to take towards my tasks
- I'd want them to give feedback and be clear about what is going well
- I'd want them to clearly communicate the good and the bad
- I'd want them to make me feel motivated
- I'd want feedback that makes me feel like I'm capable

Note 1

If it were me, what kind of leadership would I want?   **12-1-2013**

- I'd want them to make my tasks clear
- I'd want them to provide guidance on concrete actions to take towards my tasks
- I'd want them to give feedback and be clear about what is going well
- I'd want them to clearly communicate the good and the bad
- I'd want them to make me feel motivated
- I'd want feedback that makes me feel like I'm capable

The content is especially faultless. He demonstrates an exceptional understanding of how leadership should be.

However, he did not really understand why he quickly shouts at his subordinates, and why he is unable to stop himself. Nevertheless, by starting with the note "If it were me, what kind of leadership would I want?" and then writing a few more than ten pages, the following realization was born:

Shouting had become part of my method of communication. By shouting, I made my subordinates shrink back, and made myself feel terrible as well, and even though I knew all too well that nothing good comes of it, I didn't control myself, couldn't control myself.

Some titles of other notes which he wrote at the same time are:

- What kind of mentor do I want to be?
- If I were shouted at, how would I feel?
- How do those I've shouted at feel?
- At what times do I want to shout?
- After I've screamed by head off, what do I feel?
- What is an emotional outburst?

- Who do I frequently shout at?
- Who do I not shout at?

The contents of each note were deep. By taking this approach, in ten minutes time of beginning to write out these notes, he was able to obtain a deep understanding of his tendency to lose control of himself, something which had troubled him for many years.

He recognized the reasons for his actions—about which no one told him, he couldn't consult with anyone, and he himself did not know what to do—and this apparently became a big step towards improvement.

"Note-taking" is writing one page within one minute, ten pages per day. It only takes ten minutes. There's no overhead, and it has prompt effects on your mental and emotional state. Just like the aforementioned business leader, you can solve behavioral problems and even change your style.

When you continue with note-taking for three weeks to a month, words will steadily begin coming to mind. Words will well up faster than you can write them down. With things which a month prior left you feeling vague and uneasy, clear words will come to mind, and ideas will come out one after the other. Your hand won't be able to keep up with the speed of your mind, and you will feel impatient as you continue to produce.

Furthermore, if you continue for several months, you will grow able to see the complete picture instantaneously and approach "Zero Second Thinking." With certain matters, you will come to be able to instantaneously spot the issues, organize the challenges, and discern the answers. In this transformation, gender, age, and experience play no role.

The virtues of note-taking

Note-taking organizes your mind

I think that most people write notes of some sort in notebooks, on notepads, loose leaf papers, Post-it Notes, or perhaps digital notepads, Word files, and the like. Apart from things like meeting plans, thoughts and things that come to mind, things that were unpleasant, ideas about doing things a certain way, and so on—they all vary from person to person. No matter the form, when we take notes, we are less likely to carelessly forget things. To a certain extent, our thoughts also become organized.

People who have been doing this for years have likely devised all sorts of ways to go about it. They mark them up with red, blue, yellow highlighters, divide their notes from left to right. People for whom an all-encompassing method doesn't come, and who are constantly groping through various methods may also be common. I, too, spent a considerable amount of time coming up with mine, so I understand this very well.

What I would like to recommend is the method explained in the preceding section: on horizontal sheets of Letter paper, using one page each time, write a title in the upper left, and with just four to six lines per page and lines approximately ten to twenty words long, write ten pages per day, each within one minute.

By writing out notes, your vague and uneasy feelings, unresolved matters, and thoughts will be put in order. By converting your hazy feelings into words, hand-writing them, and reviewing them with your eyes, notes will become a form of external memory. By doing so, your mind will work startlingly better. Yes, the human brain does not have all that much storage capacity, so our minds don't function well when we are preoccupied with something.

Not only will your mind go to work well, but also things

you were thinking somehow or other, things you were able to do somehow or other—namely, "tacit knowledge"—will take on a definite shape. In other words, you will convert it into "explicit knowledge." You will become cognizant for the first time of exactly just how you were doing things.

If you were to ask why this is important, it is because, for example, when giving instructions to your subordinates or team members, you will be able to concretely communicate the know-how of what needs to be done as opposed to saying *well I guess do this* or *I'm not really sure but do this*. What's important to keep in mind, what must be avoided—the transfer of such know-how will become easy. When speaking with friends and superiors, too, you will grow able to converse more concretely, more sharply; communication will be smooth.

I've said it before, but I'll say it again: I believe that humans are smart. With training, everyone has a mind which can work brilliantly. While of course education is also important, with or without it people are smart. To begin with, formal education has belonged to these last hundred years or so, and prior to that humans were using their heads and living handsomely.

However, there is a problem with this innate intelligence not being capitalized on. The humans which made instantaneous judgement calls and survived the harsh conditions of nature have now attached wisdom to incompleteness, get scolded by their superiors, readily defer to their seniors, have lost confidence, and as a result their minds no longer work well.

Since humans are unable to separate their minds from their hearts, if our emotions are in disarray, our minds do not function well. We go in circles, turn back when our goal is only one step ahead, are unable to make decisions. Stress only magnifies this problem.

This is truly a waste. I want to somehow make it so that we can manifest our innate power. It's absolutely possible for our minds to work well, and it's a waste to not brandish the brilliant potential which we all possess. With this in mind, I took on this challenge from many directions.

I looked for the answers in books and held discussions with many people. I wrote in notebooks, tried writing on Letter paper, wrote on Kyoto University Style B6 index cards, used Post-it Notes, testing out every possible method. The ones I thought were good I recommended to others and had them try them out, too.

It took me many detours along the way, but ultimately, I found that note-taking on Letter paper is the most effective for organizing one's mind. I noticed that many problems could be solved with considerable ease through note-taking on Letter paper. When we take down notes, our troubles diminish to that extent. The fog clears, and the path ahead becomes easy to see. Anyone can experience the feeling of having their pent-up troubles vanish before their eyes and steadily having their mind rejuvenated and set straight one page at a time.

Note-taking builds confidence and positivity

When you take down notes, more than anything else your mind will be refreshed. You will be putting into words things that come to mind, things that you feel shaky about, so your feelings of unease will mostly disappear. In doing so, concerns about which worrying won't help, or unresolved matters that have somehow left you anxious, will be put in order, and you will come to see only that which is important. An example of this looks like Note 2 on the next page.

I had been anxious about various things regarding a project presentation, but just by writing out a single page of notes, I began to feel like this:

Ah, the thing I was most anxious about is whether or not the demo will go well. Yes, that's definitely it. Let's try it out one

Note 2

Does this project presentation look like it will go well?　　　　　**12-1-2013**

–I've done everything I had to do
–But there's one more person who I should explain
　it to in advance
–I've bounced it off of all the company's outside
　partners, there should be no problem
–Will the demo work properly?
–I'll test it out one more time tomorrow. Turns out
　the demo is really what I'm anxious about

---

more time to see if the demo will go well.

If you don't finish within one page, write out however many more pages with similar titles. Doing so will clean out your feelings of uncertainty. This takes a mere handful of minutes.

Again, a note with the title "Why I feel uneasy" can be seen at Note 3. You'll understand when you look at it, but everything is written down just as it came to mind, no scrutinizing in between. It's recorded exactly as I felt

Note 3

Why I feel uneasy   **12-1-2013**

–I've been feeling terrible all day

–Even though I never feel this way

–It could be about my section manager letting on
  about how he feels towards the new project yesterday

–If we do start the project, sure enough he might
  also participate I guess

–He probably would. If he does he will probably
  be a nuisance again

–Even though he was always quiet. This must be
  why I'm feeling weighed down

---

it, exactly as it came to me. It took less than a minute, of course. Even so, there are several realizations I wouldn't have reached had I not written them out. There's discovery. I often receive exclamations of surprise from those who have written notes—*I had never thought to write down something like this; so this is what I was thinking!*

If you regularly write out many notes like these, unexpectedly important things will become visible. What exactly is truly important, what exactly had been making you anxious, what exactly had you been trying not to get hung up on—these things will, unintentionally, inadvertently, by the time you even notice them, come out in your writing.

Unintentionally, inadvertently, by the time you even notice them—this is an important point. That which you had tried to shut your eyes to, which you had tried not to think about but in reality had made you anxious—such will become clearly visible.

Moreover, when you come to see what's important, distinguishing it from unimportant matters becomes easier, and you will naturally cease to get caught up in what's not important. This does not mean these matters will disappear, but you will begin to feel that they are not such a problem, at the very least feeling that there's no present need to be concerned over them and that even if you are concerned there's nothing to be done about it, and gradually you will become less distracted.

Once you reach this state, it will become easy to always focus on important tasks, so solving challenges will proceed smoothly. You will also postpone work less, so you will be able to take action and resolve issues before they can deteriorate. It will be harder to fall into vicious cycles. Duly, you will produce results, and self-confidence will come springing forth. Above all, not being distracted will feel stress-free and energizing.

Through note-taking, you will be able to promptly visualize the situation you've been placed in and its imminent challenges, the order of priority will in due course become clear, tasks will be swiftly resolved, you will enter a virtuous cycle, and you will naturally feel the confidence and positivity that all humans innately possess.

Note-taking releases your anger

In times when you are angry or not feeling good, writing it all out will put you at total ease. Be blunt and write out the other person's name. Suppose the other person's name is Craig. Without obscuring his name, write a note along the lines of "Why is Craig always insulting me?"

Then beyond that, continue on and straight away write out notes with titles like these:

- What is Craig feeling when he insults me?
- Who does he insult, and who does he not insult?

- How does Craig feel after he insults me?
- What's his attitude like the day after he insults me?
- Which part of me is Craig reacting to?
- What should I do in order to not make Craig angry?
- When is Craig insulting towards me?
- When I'm insulted by Craig, how do I feel?
- What did I do wrong?
- Was there something I also needed to improve on?
- What are Craig's good points, and what are his bad points?
- Could it be that Craig is short-tempered because he has an inferiority complex?
- Which friends does Craig let his guard down with? What kind of relationship do they have?
- How can I make things go better with Craig?

This is fifteen pages, fifteen minutes. Just fifteen minutes after starting, you will feel much calmer.

From those feeling poorly about something that happened at work today, etc., I definitely want for you to try writing out ten to fifteen pages like this. Boldly write out why someone would do such a horrible thing, how horrible of a person they are. Write without reservation. It doesn't mean you will be showing it to anyone. Write without even omitting names. As it were, scribble down some trash-talk.

When you do so, you will feel miraculously calmed down. In spite of having just scribbled down trash-talk, finishing writing ten to fifteen pages one page at a time will leave you feeling refreshed. At the same time, you will come to see faults of your own which were utterly invisible to you before. With things you thought were truly horrible and unforgivable, you will grow able to view them slightly more objectively. Miraculously, you will become able to do so.

I believe that the reason note-taking releases anger is because, without worrying about the public gaze, you are able to purge yourself without restraint then properly examine what you've cleaned out. It is because the outcome of this is that you will become able to take an objective point of view regarding your situation, you will grow able to see the cause of whatever has just happened, and towards this you will grasp both what should be done and what should not be done.

Some people will be able to accomplish this quickly. Everyone else will, with repetition, gradually become capable as well. You will less frequently become unreasonably angry, and your feelings will get hurt less and less.

Even in considerably difficult or chaotic situations, you will grow able to cope with composure, *without* becoming emotional.

Furthermore, with times up until now that you've felt you can't possibly listen to someone anymore, that they are unforgivable, you will grow able to see them from a slightly different viewpoint and develop a willingness to listen.

You will feel a little more centered than you did before writing notes. You will become able to view yourself objectively. In that instant, your way of dealing with someone up until then, which had been to be unintentionally belligerent, will dramatically change. You will become astonishingly calm and collected.

Of course, in cases where someone seems obviously in the wrong and is clearly holding ill will in dealing with you, it is not such an easy thing to quiet one's indignation. Even so, if you write it all out in notes—why would they do something like that, what were they thinking when they did that, are you entirely not at fault, what could you have done to prevent it—your assessment of the situation will become more accurate. Accordingly, it will be easy to devise countermeasures. And if you are able to imagine this hostile person's past trauma or sad circumstances and the like, it will be harder for the situation to turn volatile.

When it turns out like this, instead of being a clash of emotions, it will change into a far and away healthier and easier situation to address. Even in situations where the other party is in the wrong no matter how you swing it, if you write out fifteen or so pages on why they do the things they do, in imagining the circumstances of this person who can't help themself, it will become more difficult for you to get upset, and a coping method will come into view.

Incidentally, for those who no matter what cannot cope in a composed manner (*I feel sorry for him that he is unable to see from that perspective. What can I do to deal with him better?*) and instead get angry, it's common that they themselves are at fault in some way, have some insecurity or inferiority complex. They get angry because they are always having their insecurities pecked at. They perhaps have no memory of having done so themselves.

By performing note-taking, insecurities and feelings of inferiority you held up until that point will without a doubt grow weaker, so situations in which you feel anger will rapidly disappear. Feelings of anger are, in most cases, due to someone wronging you in some way or doing something you find disagreeable, but it's also due to you being unable to ward them off. Note-taking will drastically improve this.

What is critical is that there is no need to hold back. Holding back is not good for your body. It's not good for your heart either. Putting a lid on something rotten does not erase the stench. Instead, the stench will collect and grow worse. Rather than trying to bear it, it is necessary to exterminate the source of the stench. The very easy method of note-taking on Letter paper drastically relieves us of the anger and irritation that plague us.

Note-taking facilitates rapid growth

When we write notes, we become capable of organizing our minds. Being capable of organizing your mind means always having a clear grasp on what's important, what's not important, what needs to be done, and what's fine to leave as is. Even if multiple problems occur at the same time, without panicking and without getting flustered, you will be able to gather the necessary information and resolve them in order starting from the most important or serious matters.

Doing so, you will quickly produce results. The more you do it, the more you will move forward. As a result, you will feel more confident and positive, and nothing will be able to easily throw you off your game.

Even in situations that before would have made you angry, you will understand the backdrop behind others' words and actions, so you won't try to bear it, but rather will grow able to achieve serenity.

Achieving serenity means being self-confident yet humble. It means not putting up a front. Not looking down on others. Not being excessively nervous or shrinking back just because someone is of a higher position than you. Not ridiculing someone or treating them like a child just because they are of a lower position than you.

Without flying into impulsive rages or becoming emotional, it is possible to constantly remain self-possessed. However, in no way does this mean that you lack passionate sentiments. Rather, since you have a strong sense of purpose and high aspirations, it is a condition of being brimming with zeal. This is easy to say, but in reality it is exceedingly difficult to achieve. It might be a majority of people who wish to maintain serenity though are unable to do so.

Even for those achieving success within their capacity in a company, it's common for there to be forced elements arising somewhere in their work, for them to feel nervous to a greater or lesser extent with their higher-ups, subordinates, and co-workers. There is a distinct split between those who take the very best measures while maintaining serenity through note-taking and those who do not. This is because of the accumulative positive effect of optimal measures, and because there is a big difference in the approaches of each when tackling difficult situations.

By taking notes, it is possible to shoot to achieve your objectives while leveraging the skills of your teammates and treating others with respect. As such, needless clashes will decrease, and it becomes possible to naturally carry out teamwork.

Having done so, you will gain more confidence, and the virtuous cycle will continue. You will experience growth more than ever before, even to a surprising extent. Your mind will be constantly organized, so you will less frequently get caught in the current of your emotions. You will be able to see the broader picture, so you will be able to discern what needs to be done right away and what to prepare for next, and you will proceed to carry out work on a larger scale.

For example, if you are a new employee, anything and everything at work is a first, likely putting you constantly on edge. During this time, it's fine to write twenty to thirty pages per day on things you notice, things you feel, things you've been cautioned about, things about which you've thought *this time for sure*. It is likely that these will not possibly fit within ten pages, but even then it will only take twenty to thirty minutes a day. I want you to try this out, because with just that, your worries will sharply decrease and your aptitude for your work will visibly improve.

I've received feedback from many people that within a mere three or four weeks of starting note-taking, they became able to firmly grasp the remarks of others at meetings, had their own remarks given more attention than before, and had their ideas adopted by others. Note-taking is an effective method for experiencing growth at one's job.

Chapter 3

The Note-taking Method for Cultivating Zero Second Thinking

When taking notes on horizontal Letter paper, write a title in the upper left and underline it. It is just that simple. Not in a notebook, not on a computer, not on cards, not on a small note pad—on Letter paper. Moreover, rather than cramming a page full, write just four to six lines then be done with it. This can be written in the blink of an eye, so it will not feel burdensome. Because it's on Letter paper, you can write out not just words but also pictures and diagrams with ease. There's also no need to worry about spacing and the size of your handwriting.

The reason for turning the paper horizontal is that between current challenges and solutions strategies, and issues up until then and their responses, it will become common to represent the flow of time. I of course tried leaving papers vertical, but it is easier on horizontal sheets to clearly achieve this representation.

The reason for underlining titles is to make them stand out. Titles and the four to six lines beneath them will be clearly demarcated. On programs like PowerPoint we would make the font size larger, but when writing by hand, a quick underlining will get the job done.

In the upper right, put the date. I write in the abbreviated style of "1-23-2014." I do this because it is the easiest to see and takes little time to write. What's important in note-taking is writing the title, date, and content on one page within one minute, so there is no leeway to write out things like the name of the month.

How to write titles

For a title (which is the theme of the note), anything is fine. Without hesitating, write out whatever comes to mind as is. This can look something like this:

Titles related to work

- How can I work faster?
- Times when I can work well/times when I can't
- When is my work interrupted?
- How can I swiftly finalize proposals?
- What I will finish today and tomorrow
- Preparation for next week's meeting
- How to communicate with my higher-ups
- For improving communication with other divisions?
- What I want to do if I become section manager
- What are my strengths? How can I strengthen them further?

Titles related to studying English

- How can I continue to study English for thirty minutes every day?

- For discerning the difference between *L* and *R*?
- For pronouncing *L* cleanly?
- For acquiring good pronunciation?
- How can I improve my vocabulary?
- Is memorizing 3000 words good enough?
- What can I do to prepare for the TOEIC exam?
- In what ways will using the TOEIC exam strengthen my English ability?
- For strengthening my listening skills over a short period of time?
- How can I properly utilize both dramas and podcasts that are in English?

Titles related to the future

- What do I truly want to do?
- What am I truly good at?
- What am I suited to? What can I truly do well?
- How to separate what I'm doing right now from activities geared towards my future?
- For producing maximum results now while thinking of my future?
- How can I sort out my vision for the future?
- Taking my future into consideration, what is the most important thing to do now?
- How to prepare for a career change?

- The merits and demerits of a career change?
- What to confirm with my seniors about changing careers

Titles related to reading

- What kind of books do I want to read?
- How can I strike a balance in the books I read?
- What books will I read in this coming year?
- After reading them, how can I make them useful?
- How can I sort my impressions and make practical use of them?
- For making practical use of even just half of the knowledge/know-how I gleaned from reading?
- For increasing my reading speed?
- What can I do to read one book in two days?
- Books I recommend to others
- How to effectively recommend them?

Titles related to time management

- To do by next week
- What to absolutely implement this month
- For implementing without fail what I've chosen?
- How to make an order of priority?
- What to do in order to not waste time
- How do people who work fast shorten their time spent?

- What to cut to economize my time?
- What are the circumstances when I feel highly productive? How can I expand those?
- For waking up an hour earlier in the morning?
- For becoming a bit more of a morning person?

Titles related to taking care of your health

- For taking care of my physical health?
- For not skipping breakfast?
- How can I be sure to stick to a diet this time?
- This week's dinner menu
- Ways to avoiding catching a cold
- How can I guarantee that I get enough sleep?
- What are the most effective times to go to sleep and wake up?
- For not waking up in the middle of the night?
- For thoroughly waking myself up in the morning?
- Is it possible to do things like make the curtains open automatically at 6 AM?

Titles related to your private life}

- How can I make my communication with him/her go smoother?
- What is he/she interested in?
- What can I do to make them look my way more?

- What can I do to talk in a kinder way?
- What can I do to better ask about their concerns?
- Should we go out somewhere together this weekend?
- How can we meet in the middle on what each of us wants to do?
- Is there no way for us to stop fighting?
- How can I make work and my private life coexist?
- How do I relate with my middle and high school friends?

In this way, you make the words that come to your mind into titles themselves. There's no reason to think hard on them. You *must not* think hard on them. These are not anything you will show to others, so write the phrases that come to mind as is in the upper left of sheets of Letter paper.

It's fine whether they are in the form of questions or of phrases beginning like "ways to…." However, I feel that questions are slightly easier to write out. Here I've written seventy examples, but it's common for them to come out as questions.

Writing similar titles many times over

Even if you write a certain title today, there are times when tomorrow the same or similar words and phrases will come to mind. In that case, without hesitating, write them once more. There's no need to re-examine what you wrote yesterday. Without reviewing, write it again exactly as it comes to your mind. If three days later a similar title strikes you again, use it to write a note. Without looking back, write it down earnestly.

When you write one down many times over and reach a state of mental order, it will stop occurring to you to write more regarding that title (or theme). This is because what you are hung up on, as well as your efforts to deal with it, will become clear, and the need for deliberately taking notes on it will go away.

For example, when I first entered McKinsey, I was taught by my team leader one after another about things like how to summarize interviews, methods of analysis, and the work of client team management. Trying in my own way to assimilate it all, I wrote notes with all of my might. At this time, just regarding interviews alone, I wrote notes with titles like these:

- How do I summarize the outcome of an interview?
- What can I do to swiftly summarize the outcome of an interview?
- For smoothly making records during an interview?
- For putting important points on a chart while carrying out an interview?
- For getting to the bottom of especially critical points during an interview?
- For immediately summarizing after an interview ends?
- How to summarize the outcome of an interview
- For quickly summarizing the outcome of an interview and producing a written report?
- For smoothly carrying out an interview and quickly summarizing it?

These were not written in one sitting, but rather over the span of a few weeks to a few months, written right when they occurred to me. They're all similar titles, so there are likely many people who think there's no need to write them so many times. In reality I, too, have many times over quit this method and tried to find previously written notes to add to them.

Nevertheless, in trying this out for real, I noticed that this way of going about it made it difficult to organize my mind, or rather that it made it difficult to explore for and internalize the best solutions. Notes are, in the first place, not something you carry around with you, so you won't find them right away. Even if they are in your home office, it is not easy to find the note you are looking for in one to two seconds. In the time you spend looking here and there, the flash of inspiration you had will disappear somewhere—an opportunity squandered.

At any rate, these are to be written in one minute, so it is more efficient to write them down fresh without looking at things you've written before.

Moreover, upon looking back later on, it became clear that I had become able to write material much superior to that which I had written early on. I believe that the process of every time putting into words what came to mind, writing it out by hand, confirming it visually, and polishing as I wrote was an exceptional form of organization.

In this way, in the span of writing five to ten or even twenty pages on more or less the same theme, you will come to feel that you've exhausted what you can think and write about that theme. A big transformation will be taking place in your heart. At this point in time, it will cease to be a challenge which you need to consider and write on anymore. You will be in a state of more than ample mental orderliness, able to lay your hands on a clear vision.

How to save up titles

There are those for whom note titles do not readily come to mind. I recommend in this situation to, just as in Note 4, on a horizontal sheet of Letter paper, draw roughly three vertical lines at evenly spaced intervals, then list out every note title you can think of.

When note titles come, they come all at once. For example, if you think of the title "How to communicate with Sergio" then it's fine to write out the same title for seven or eight more people.

And again, differentiating by circumstance, instead of just "How to communicate with Sergio," titles like "How to communicate with Sergio when he's in a bad mood," or "How to communicate with Sergio when he's sad," or "How to communicate with Sergio when we're out for drinks" will also come to mind.

If you prepare a hundred titles on one page, then when none come to mind, you will be able to continue note-taking without strain.

Note 4

Note Titles	**12-1-2013**

–How to communicate with Sergio

–How to communicate with Craig

–How to communicate with Amy

–How to communicate with my

  section manager

–How to communicate with Jeremy

–How to communicate with Vanessa

–How to communicate with Sergio

  when he's in a bad mood

–How to communicate with Sergio

  when he's sad

–How to communicate with Sergio

  when we're out for drinks

–For leading meetings well

–For effectively ending meetings

  on time?

–For being certain to prepare for

  meetings

–What should I do when my

  opinion is met with opposition at

  a meeting?

–For using the whiteboard well at

  meetings?

–For having others speak up more

  in meetings?

–For reliably having others imple-

  ment matters mutually agreed

  upon in meetings?

–For quickly replying to emails?

–When am I able to quickly reply

  to emails?

–When do I fail to reply to emails in

  a timely manner?

How to write the main text

Notes consist of a title, four to six lines of main text (ten to twenty words per line), and a date—all written within one minute. Write what comes to mind as it comes without any excessive consideration. Write it just as you felt it. No thinking of difficult things. No thinking of composition, either. No selecting words; just thoughts as they come.

There are those for whom only one or two lines will come out, but this is no cause for concern. You will soon be able to write out more, so I want for you to just try for it. When I teach note-taking, I have students look at a clock to get a grasp on how long a minute is, on how quickly they need to hurry. They are always surprised because, done in this way, they become capable of writing one page within one minute before they've even written ten pages. The number of words itself will go on to increase.

Each line begins with a dash (—) and aligns with the left, just like the example below. This left-alignment is because there are times when writing will be added on the right side as well (see page 201).

As for word size and line spacing, the balance of the pho-

Note 5

How to write notes   **12-1-2013**

–Write note titles in the upper left
–Four to six lines, write the main text like this
–Write one page within one minute
–Just write well enough that you can read it
–Write thoroughly enough, about half of this page

---

to at right is good for Letter paper. Note 5 features the same content but typed out. I want for you to write with this balance. If you write smaller than this, notes will be somewhat difficult to see at a glance or when you line them up on a desk (I elaborate on this later on), and if you write larger than this, four to six lines will take up most of the page, making it difficult to freely add pictures or figures. Moreover, having gotten used to writing large, you will run out of space in cases where it actually becomes necessary to write larger. It will become difficult to feel carefree and not make omissions as you record whatever comes to your mind.

Stretching out each line

For each line, if they are too short, they will not be sufficiently concrete nor be good practice in verbalizing the hazy feelings in your mind. So, I recommend using ten to twenty words per line. At this length, they will have a more or less sufficient substance to them.

Note 6 features extremely short lines at around two to four words each. With people like this, upon inquiring whether they are unable to write any more, that is absolutely not the case. It is the majority of people who, upon being asked individually, are capable of explaining more in depth. In other words, they are simply not writing thoroughly.

This is such a waste. A waste because it is a missed opportunity to successfully express what is in one's mind, to put one's concerns and ideas into a tangible form.

For example, with just "Decide on an agenda," it's not clear what to do after deciding. It's also unclear when and what the agenda is for. With just "Distribute materials," it is unclear how to distribute them and what to do upon distributing them. With "Shorten remarks," the gist of it makes sense, but there's no concrete plan for how to actualize it. With "Make use of whiteboard," it's unclear for what this person wants to use the whiteboard.

Accordingly, I recommend writing notes like Note 7 rather than Note 6.

Note 6

<table>
<tr><td><u>In order to curtail meeting time</u></td><td>12-1-2013</td></tr>
</table>

—Decide on an agenda

—Distribute materials

—Shorten remarks

—Make use of whiteboard

Bad example: Because the sentences are too short, they lack concreteness

Done like this, the aforementioned ambiguities will disappear, making for notes that are far and away more concrete than Note 6. At ten to twenty words, each line will stretch to between two thirds and three fourths of the horizontal length of a sheet of paper. Only after starting with this format can you record the feelings, ideas, and

Note 7

In order to curtail meeting time	12-1-2013

–Properly choose the meeting agenda, then send it to others beforehand and establish expectations

–Distribute necessary materials for meetings at least a day in advance, and cut explanation time in half

–Urge everyone again to extract the main point from their remarks before speaking

–Eliminate redundancy by writing discussion contents on the whiteboard

Good example: Sentences are sufficiently long and concrete; contents are clear challenges that come to mind with sufficient concreteness and accuracy.

There are some who cannot write this much at first, but this is absolutely no cause for concern. You will soon become able to do so. It is just recording, as is, whatever comes to your mind alongside the title of each page.

Working hard to write four to six lines

As a general rule, the main text of notes is four to six lines, but in the beginning, there are times when nothing comes to mind no matter what you do. In these situations, it is good to work hard to write three lines. I've had over a thousand people practice note-taking, and with a little effort anyone can do it. Everyone, without fail, has something on their mind. It is simply a matter of writing that down. Even those who are not used to it become capable over the course of writing twenty to thirty pages.

Women seem to have extremely strong communication abilities, with many taking to it from the second they begin note-taking. Even just watching them write makes it look incredibly fun. It's as though ideas keep flowing out, enough to make you think that they might continue writing forever if left to their own devices. Strangely enough, there aren't many exceptions to this.

On the other hand, roughly a third of men struggle a bit just in the beginning. There are even some who work hard to produce two short lines. However, when I introduce note-taking in workshops and have them write out ten pages on the spot, all of them become able within their capacity to write them. Even if they can only write a small amount, by not giving up and keeping their eye on the clock while trying to write one page in one minute, they quickly improve.

There is a reason for writing the main text in four to six lines. When you write out whatever comes to mind in response to the title you've thought of, it generally ends up being four lines or more. It is rare to end at three lines. I like to think that because complete narrative structures tend to feature an introduction, rising action, climax, and resolution, we end up wanting that fourth line.

Well then, why stop when you have six lines? This is in order to keep your mind constantly organized. If you continue to write endlessly, you will end up stringing together important things with unimportant ones. You are also liable to steadily write out things of a different caliber. So, I recommend writing until a maximum of six lines, even if you want to write more. When you want to write more, it is surely a subpoint belonging to some larger point.

In other words, if the four important points you plan to write out occur to you in the order of A, B, C, and D, then write them as follows:

–A
–B
–C
–D

Strangely, this will become an important order. This is because things you are concerned about will occur to you first. It's not common for things you aren't concerned about to come to mind first. Put another way, in most cases, by writing in the order they strike you, you will be able to write out the essential points. This is because the human mind is well-crafted.

Since you only have one minute, trying to write out ten to twenty words per line, most people will be able to write four lines, and those who write well five or six. It's also true that setting a time limit at one minute is designed to discourage coming up with extraneous matters.

Seldomly, there are people who can write with staggering momentum. Despite the time limit of one minute, there are those who end up being able to write out seven to ten lines. In cases where someone comes to want to write in this way, it is common for the degrees of importance to be in disarray. Below is a conceptual explanation of this:

```
–A
–B1
–B2
–C
–D1
–D2
–D3
–D4
```

In other words, although it was imperative to write out A, B, C, and D, which are originally of the same level, B and D are addressed at a lower level.

For example, in the following way, states and cities are jumbled up together:

```
–Maine
–Seattle
–Tacoma
–Colorado
```

—Miami

—Orlando

—Tampa

—Jacksonville

With states and cities this is blatantly obvious, but there are cases in which the difference in level is not so readily apparent. However, with a little care, you will cease to confuse them. Even writing quickly, you will become able to swiftly write out points of the same level.

In that regard, in the beginning, I recommend staying within four lines or above up to a maximum of six lines. This is because when you try to write out too much, your attention to and sense for differences in degree of importance will become diluted.

Those who write out seven to ten lines within one minute are considerably quick thinkers who can swiftly verbalize what comes to their minds, but it's common for them to also be weak at thinking in a structurally organized way, so please be aware of this. Being weak at thinking in a structurally organized way translates to not habitually considering what is and is not important nor an order of priority.

Nevertheless, it is common for this type of person to

not grasp this point even if they have it pointed out to them. It's as though something doesn't click. In such cases, I recommend the following structure:

–A
–B
  •B1
  •B2
–C
–D
  •D1
  •D2
  •D3
  •D4

I recommend note-taking be done in this form of ranking items A, B, C, and D of top importance (since they begin with a dash, I call them "dash points") and within each adding particulars (since these begin with dots, I call them "dot points").

To give an example, see Note 8 on page 116. To begin with, it's an ordinary note with four to six lines.

By contrast, adding in dot points turns it into Note 9 from the previous page. Lines one, two, and four are

Note 8

In order to give positive feedback　　**12-1-2013**

—I want to give even more positive feedback

—I'll try to at least five times or more every day.
Thirty times in five days from Mon-Fri

—Blend together praise, shows of appreciation, and
suggestions

—I'm anxious as to whether I can do this well, but
oh well, I'll try it out. If I do so I'll see results sooner or later

---

supplemented with two each. Through these, who they will give positive feedback to and how they will put this into practice five times or more every day is concretely mentioned. Also mentioned is the feeling of wanting to try without delay because of the lack of risk involved.

Not minding the order in which you write

Do not give a second thought as to the structure and order in which you write your four to six lines. If you consider things like having a quadripartite narrative structure, or

Note 9

<u>In order to give positive feedback</u>   **12-1-2013**

—I want to give even more positive feedback
  • To team members
  • To members of collaborative partner companies
—I'll try to at least five times or more every day.
  Thirty times in five days from Mon-Fri
  • Two times in the morning, three times in the
    afternoon
  • If possible, on the weekends too, four times
    per day
—Blend together praise, shows of appreciation, and
  suggestions
—I'm anxious as to whether I can do this well, but oh well,
  I'll try it out. If I do so I'll see results sooner or later
  • Even if I can't do it well, there's no risk
  • It's something I've been meaning to try for a
    while, so it'd be nice to try

> A more detailed way of writing: Between four to six
> main lines, several lines of subpoints (represented
> after bullet points) (this is only for times when you
> want to write particularly detailed notes)

---

practicing inductive or deductive reasoning, your thinking will abruptly slow down.

Strangely enough, just by hastily jotting down your thoughts, you will naturally become able to write in quadripartite narrative structures and with easily understood sequencing. You will likely achieve this in forty to fifty pages (which is four or five days).

The good news is that just by writing enough, you will naturally grow capable, without strain or exertion.

Human ability is inherently substantial. We lose our ability to be effective the moment we think we need to do something, to follow some rule, to keep up appearances. It's because we try to behave smartly that the brakes get put on.

The note-taking that I recommend might have the effect of continuing to persuade you, ten times or more every day, that it is okay to not put up a front, okay to release whatever comes to mind as is.

Following the note-taking format without fail

When I explain note-taking and have others practice it, it always maintains an exceptional reputation. *This is revelatory; From now on I will write them every day!* —such are the reactions I frequently receive. Even so, while their enthusiasm is great, there is *always* someone who tries orienting their sheet of Letter paper vertically, or tries using a notebook, or tries splitting the page in half and writing in sections, or in some other way tinkers with the format. There is always someone who puts their effort not into writing hundreds of pages, but rather into proceeding in directions I have not requested, especially ones I have recommended against.

The "note-taking" which I explain in this book is a method of a considerably high degree of perfection, a method reached after I myself tried a large number of others and then wrote tens of thousands of pages after settling on this one. It doesn't look like much at a glance, but it is packed with practical ideas. Doing away with an understanding of this background and instead scheming in roundabout, trivial ways will lead to the valuable know-how I've created not being put to effective use.

First of all, rather than tinkering with the format, I want for you to pour your energy into the content. Upon writing several hundred pages, I believe that you will be convinced of the reasoning behind the current format. It is a product of having had close to a thousand people weigh in as well, so for now I want for you to work hard on the content-side of things.

This is the same as having just begun learning to play tennis or golf or piano. Wanting to hold the club or racket a certain way, not knowing why but wanting to swing it a certain way, wanting a racket twice the size, wanting to play the piano with only four fingers—although one might say it looks cool, there's mostly no future in it.

Those who will truly grow will obediently take it all in, and once they reach a certain level will naturally keep aiming higher.

Writing whatever comes to mind

You now know the format for writing notes. Well then, concretely speaking, *what* do you write in them?

Things that strike you, things you are hung up on, doubts, what you need to do next, challenges in your growth, infuriating things you cannot forgive—write whatever comes to mind. Just record phrases exactly as they come to mind.

It's not something you will show to others, so in titles and in the main text, too, write down the names of people you hate without obscuring them. The more you write everything concretely, the more you will be able to write without blurring your focus. Holding back is forbidden. By writing frankly, you will feel refreshed, as though you have cleaned out the garbage from your room. Your heart will be kept tidy and orderly, and by fixing your gaze on exactly *what* is troubling you, your troubles will also drastically diminish.

Things we hate, things we are anxious about, things which make us angry but about which we don't know what to do—these things torment us.

Scenes of awful experiences arise and disappear, disappear and arise. The more negative something was, the worse it feels and the harder we try to not think about it. Even with effort, unpleasant things stay unpleasant, so they come floating back at unexpected times. We want to disappear them once and for all with an eraser. But, so far we have not been able to wipe clean the contents of our minds (regarding truly horrific circumstances, it is possible for our brains to erase memories. However, they do not truly disappear and instead remain as deep wounds, so as trauma they restrict our behavior at every turn).

Still, when we write out what plagues us—on Letter paper, one sheet, one minute each time—our emotional scars will heal little by little, just as though we are disappearing them with an eraser one by one. The anguish and hurt in our hearts will abate. It is a feeling of dredging out the sludge within our hearts.

Towards things which you believe you must not think about but end up doing so anyway, instead by clearly including the name of the person you dislike as you write down on a paper before your eyes, your feelings will miraculously subside. This has a bigger effect than complaining to a friend for three hours does.

The reason is because by concretely writing out their name on a sheet of paper in front of you, along with *what* you dislike about them, *how* they are horrible, *to what extent* they are a bad person, *why* you were unable to object to them, and *how* you will prove yourself superior, you will be able to firmly fix your gaze on your own feelings. It is because by doing so, you will be able to put things in order better than you would by just simply talking, you will stop moving in circles, and you will be able to more quickly sort out your emotions. Fixing onto paper the unpleasant or unforgivable aspects of someone which would have bothered you ten times over had you not written them out, you will be able to move onward.

If done on a piece of paper in front of you when you're all alone, it is possible to write out things from the darkest regions of your heart, things you cannot tell even your best friend. This is because there's no concern that anyone will question what kind of person you are. You will become fully honest with your own emotions.

After you've spilled everything into your notes, while looking at them, you can freshly write more notes on things that come to mind, things which you ultimately can't forgive, the part of that person you hate most, and so on. With truly infuriating experiences, it's good to keep on writing indefinitely—even hundreds of pages.

You will understand once you try it, but the truth is doing so won't be necessary. If you write twenty to thirty pages, you will likely realize you cannot write much more on that. Around the time you realize this, you will to an extent become able to view your emotions and circumstances in an objective way and come to feel considerably composed. From there, you will begin to notice where you were in the wrong and begin to feel, even if just a little bit, that you know the right way forward. If you are writing one page per minute, reaching this point takes roughly thirty minutes. However much time you spend, even if you spend an hour, you will feel remarkably different.

Writing notes on the back of used Letter paper

When writing notes, it is best to use the reverse side of used Letter paper. Use the blank back side of unneeded documents. If it's used paper, you will not hesitate to churn out notes. You will be able to proceed writing without holding back. You'll understand if you try writing four to six lines on a fresh sheet of paper, but you will probably feel daunted at the prospect of continuing writing such a small amount on ten to twenty pages every single day. If it's the back of used paper, you will not mind in the slightest.

If by no means can you procure appropriate used paper, then using the 500-sheet packets of copy paper sold at online office supply stores and the like will cost roughly three to four dollars, which means less than one cent per sheet, totaling less than ten cents per day. Buying one packet is enough for a month and a half. It might be bothersome how clean they are, but they are definitely not expensive. Moreover, the invigorating feeling of completing a bundle of 500 notes will be amazing.

In cases where you don't really have immediate access to used paper, I recommend the following method of procuring it while becoming more attuned to new information.

For those with the ambition to grow, I recommend spending thirty minutes every day on gathering information online. Concretely speaking, it is good to scan articles generated by content curation tools on your Facebook or Twitter timelines (the posts which pop up in succession after logging in), in email magazines, Gunosy, Crowsnest, and the like. For those who have yet to begin using Facebook and Twitter, I believe it best to begin, for beyond having become almost indispensable tools for information gathering, they have also come to substitute for email as communication tools. It is just as after the telephone was invented, when utilizing them expanded one's world more than could be done without.

Content curation tools supply recommended articles selected every day from popular articles on Facebook, Twitter, etc., and from keywords pertaining to your interests. Based on which articles you read within these, they use that information to provide even more personalized articles.

In my case, when I come across a good article, I scan over all of the articles written by that blogger or journalist. This is because a blogger or journalist who has written a good article has an extraordinarily high likelihood of producing other in-depth articles.

In doing so, although you will skip over the majority of articles, it is good to print out ones that you think are especially important. By having them in-hand and high-lighting and annotating while reading, you will be able to grasp important content more deeply, to make it your own. The aptitude for acquiring information gained through doing so is something that using things like bookmarks and Evernote cannot possibly imitate.

After highlighting and annotating, file them in with your notes in clear folders according to theme (I explain how to use folders in Chapter 5).

Here I will at last return back to my original train of thought, but in most cases when you print out articles, more than a few pages of advertisements and whatnot appear at the end. It's difficult to check what page the article runs to and where the advertisements start, and since doing so only costs time, I print them out without giving it a second thought. Those sheets will become reverse sides suited for notes. Of course, I also frequently utilize the reverse side of old Letter documents.

Nowadays, because black and white laser printers cost about eighty dollars and print exceptionally fast, I recommend them alongside note-taking. The unit cost for each printing is also considerably cheaper than with inkjet printers, so I believe that they are an almost indispensable tool for anyone trying to do their best at work.

Writing ten pages every day

I recommend writing ten notes every day. Since one page takes one minute to write, this only costs ten minutes per day. Furthermore, you won't be writing them all in one go, but rather quickly the moment they occur to you. By recording your thoughts the moment they occur to you, your mind will function better, and moreover this will stimulate new ideas, so it is better to not try to write them down all in one go after the fact. You will forget what thoughts occurred to you in the first place, so if you are to record them, it is better to jot down a single one-page note at a time.

Writing ten pages each day sounds like no big deal, and I'm sure many people can write as much. However, when this becomes thirty pages in three days, or seventy pages in a week, exhaustion begins to surface. Those without a great desire to improve themselves tend to drop out.

As a guest speaker several times every month, I recommend note-taking, and many people actually try it out. The majority of them are elated, telling me they definitely want to continue writing.

Even so, those who actually continue to write are unfortunately in the minority. At ten pages per day, this becomes 140 pages in two weeks, 300 pages in a month, and 1800 pages in half a year. Though they are simple notes which take a mere minute to write, even at just that they will become something tremendous.

By just taking ten minutes each day to write ten pages of notes, within three weeks anyone can feel considerable effects and personal growth—more than before, you will more easily comprehend everything others say at meetings; others will listen better to your own remarks; you will grow able to fully hear others out without getting flustered; somehow you will be more confident than before; and so on.

Why not five pages, or twenty pages, but *ten* pages? Of course, I tried it all. There are, rarely, cases when I want to write twenty to thirty pages, but I noticed that if I write on average ten pages each day, I can roughly cover everything that concerned or struck me that day. Naturally, I would be having more thoughts than this, but because the more I wrote the more organized my mind became, averaging ten notes per day became satisfactory. At any rate, if you continue on to write seventy notes in one week, with one page per note, certain meanings and concerns will be exhausted. Your supply of new ideas will also be exhausted. If you continue to purge yourself of the anxieties that are slowing down your thinking, without a doubt you will come to feel like writing ten pages a day is good enough.

There are also probably those thinking that *no, that's ridiculous, every day I have dozens of things I'm thinking of, an inexhaustible supply of ideas welling up, and unresolved questions coming about one after another*. If this is you, it is absolutely fine to write thirty or even forty pages a day. That as it stands is an amazing thing.

Yet, if you try this out for real, it probably won't continue all that long. Writing ten pages per day—in other words, on ten different themes—is ultimately quite a difficult task. Two or three days is good, but most people do not continue writing ten pages a day for even a week.

Why? I dare say that be it as it may that one is ordinarily thinking of many things, the majority are redundancies, repetitions, and hesitations. If you write those out one page for each, that matter will tentatively be brought to an end, so matters which you need to worry over and contemplate will rapidly decrease. Because you are leaving them in your head, you might think that you have all kinds of thoughts and ideas every day, but in reality that is probably not the case. Coming up with ten fresh worries or challenges day after day is no trivial matter.

Conversely, without writing them onto notes, you'll continue thinking *maybe it's this or maybe it's that* about the same old things, and so it serves as proof that your troubles won't diminish, that you are wasting your smarts, and that you are throwing away your time.

Immediately writing one page in one minute

In the main text of notes, you can either list out problematic issues or ideas and the like, or write in stories like those with quadripartite narrative structures. With either one, it is best to just write it out without worrying or overthinking. Write what comes to your mind just as is. Without contemplating this or that, write it out just as you feel it. In the beginning, while watching the clock, finish writing four to six lines on a page within one minute. Even in times when you want to top it up with just a little more writing, only elongate your time by about fifteen seconds in making this exception.

Allowing one page per minute is because if there's no rush, three or five minutes will pass in the blink of an eye. Most people probably have an experience of sitting before a sheet of paper and finding something to think about for however long. There are likely few people who do not have an experience of writing two or three lines then tearing it up and throwing it away, grumbling to themselves and writing a bit more before tearing that up and throwing it away, too.

The problem is, spending enough time on something does not necessarily mean it will turn out well. Whether it's with a composition or a proposal, most people have experienced their productivity skyrocket just before a deadline. Human minds and hearts are different from computers, and are incredibly dependent on environmental circumstances.

In particular, it is definitely not true with one-page notes that leisurely spending time on them will create a significantly better product. I've had many people try out note-taking, but if I don't say anything, many minutes pass in the blink of an eye without translating to increased output. Time spent at a loss and hesitating only increases. If that's the case, quickly finishing writing and moving on to the next will be much more conducive to mental organization. It will be practice in verbalizing feelings of unease, and productivity will increase as well.

However, just because you are hurrying, that absolutely does not mean it is fine to write in crude, inaccurate

English. In reality, with just a little effort, you will become able to instantly write clear and correct English. Anyone is capable of this in conversation:

"Good morning. How was the debriefing session yester-day?"
"Thanks, it went well."
"That's good. Did the department head give you the OK?"
"Yeah, she was really into it. So much so that I was even a little surprised."
"Really. I wonder what part she liked."
"She seemed to appreciate that I really listened to what users are saying."
"That's great. Teach me the ropes for user interviews next time, yeah?"

Conversations like these happen in a flash. Done fast, they're probably about fifteen seconds. There's no way they take a whole minute. Moreover, it's impeccable, perfect English. Everyone is equipped with this ability.

Even so, when we have a paper or maybe a computer in front of us, this capacity drops tenfold. Note-taking changes this. Changes this from the root. The impetus for this is the sense of speed at one page per minute.

Writing carefully and neatly costs time, so just neat

enough that you can read it is fine. Notes are something you write for your own sake, but once you get used to them you can also copy and distribute them to your team members or, in some cases, use them to explain things to your higher-ups. For that purpose, rather than using frantic scribbles, it is best to add in practice for roughly considering the appearance and balance, too. This will be easier for you to read as well. To begin with, whether you write neatly or sloppily, the fact is that the time spent will not change very much.

In the note-taking workshops which I frequently hold, I explain the aim behind note-taking, move straight into explaining how to write them, then soon have participants write their own. There are plenty who during their first time labor to produce two to three lines, or who only write two to five words per line.

However, upon having them write out several pages, they speed up surprisingly fast. The gears in their mind steadily begin to click. In the space of writing five or seven pages, they become able to write down the contents of their minds without much strain. Taking a look to compare each participant's first page with one several pages later, the difference is pronounced. The difference in length and number of lines greatly widens.

In the beginning, I really want for you to write while

watching the minute hand of a clock, being sure to finish at one minute. A title, the date, and four to six lines of main text. After beginning, you will relatively soon acquire a sense of how long a minute lasts. There are those for whom the outset is a tad painful, but have just a little patience. With it, you will improve so rapidly that you will wonder what your stumbling in the beginning was all about. Just like that, anyone can become able to write notes.

Even after you have become able to write a page in one minute, you might sometimes feel that you want to write in just a bit more. In that case, while maintaining your sense of speed, allocating fifteen more seconds to append what you'd like to write in is fine. Once you've grown accustomed to writing swiftly, this extended fifteen seconds will be extraordinarily precious. Your brain is moving at hyperspeed during these fifteen seconds. Done like this, your sense of time and of speed will become increasingly fine-tuned.

Directly after writing a note, spend two or three seconds polishing it. It's also fine to review each previous line as soon as you've written it. If there's a word you'd like to add, without hesitating insert it with an arrow. However, once you get in the groove, this time will cease to be very necessary. This is because you will become able to write neither too much nor too little, with the most fitting words coming to mind instantly.

Once you get used to note-taking, there will mostly not be any need to polish your notes, for you will always be writing concrete material, starting from what is most important. There will even be times when what you've written is so elegant that you will question who wrote it. On the other hand, when you create things like Power-Point materials based on your notes, polishing them will naturally be part of the process. On such occasions, while looking at your notes, feel around for the most suitable phrasing.

Another important point is to write notes on the spot the very moment they occur to you. As a general rule, rather than ten pages all in one go before you sleep at night, it's the moment they strike you. When something has caught your interest, record it in writing before you forget. This way allows you to write with the freshest emotion possible.

I believe that each idea is a once-in-a-lifetime encounter. Because you may not meet with the same idea or concern twice, you should record them in writing then and there. When you record them, they will no longer disappear. They will take hold, become yours. In spite of being something you've written yourself, there will likely be many times upon looking back that you feel impressed by what you've produced.

If you try to write ten pages of notes all in one go right before bed, memories of content you should have hit upon have flown away. Even if you dimly remember, the content will become ambiguous. Because this makes it hard to write in note form, and because writing them will gradually come to feel bothersome, I do not recommend it. Simply put, it will *always* be better to record your thoughts then and there as soon as they occur to you. In that situation, writing one page frankly only requires one minute. As such, while they might end up being short sentences, it's common to be able to do this in thirty to forty seconds, so it's something that can be done satisfactorily even during meetings.

As soon as they occur to you means at any time— right after you wake up, during your commute, right after you arrive at work, during your lunch break, during work, right before bed, and so on. The moment something crosses your mind is best. In my case, ideas occur to me in situations where I don't have much else to do, as when on a flight or the bullet train. Since ancient times, it has been said that the "three ons" (on the horse, on the pillow, and on the toilet) are the best times to elaborate on ideas when writing a composition, but it really is just like that.

Why it's wrong to use notebooks, diaries, Microsoft Word, etc.

If you continue to take notes, your mind will feel astonishingly refreshed. Stress will go away. Without worrying about anything, just record what comes to your mind. Since each subject concludes in one page, you do not need to worry about context nor feel bound by form. Record it all just as it comes. It's like cleaning up trash from the floor of a room—no worrying about the order in which you pick it up, but rather just a clean sweep of it all.

You will not use any energy in organizing or systematizing. This is huge. It is the biggest factor that will dramatically increase your productivity and make it possible to demonstrate your highest ability. That writing proposals takes so much time and energy is because between thinking we must write lucidly and trying to implement structure, we become stressed and our thinking becomes dull. The average person wastes an enormous amount of time. If done on a note on Letter paper, it is simply a matter of expelling it all out without thinking or worrying about anything at all.

People who use notebooks as organizational tools are presumably numerous, but I do not really recommend it. I myself in the beginning wrote in notebooks. However, by continuing to write my thoughts and concerns as they came to me, a whole notebook would soon be filled. As I was writing a steady amount, before I knew it I had used up as many as twenty notebooks.

More than anything the problem is that while they are good for writing down your thoughts, it is impossible to then sort them. Since I could only accumulate my writings in chronological order, it was impossible to rearrange them when I wrote on something similar several days or weeks later. In the end, I made it so I could search by inserting different-colored Post-it Notes—yellow ones on pages I wrote about how to conduct interviews, blue ones on pages about reading, pink ones on pages about communication. Nevertheless, with this method, the Post-it Notes piled up like a mountain, and I could only create as many categories as there are colors of Post-its. Before long, I was even writing subheadings on yellow Post-its, and increasingly I could not bring it under control.

I also cannot recommend diaries for the same reason. First of all, just as with notebooks, sorting is impossible.

Furthermore, by nature, diaries are conducive to writing in chronological order. It may be due to linking bad memories to exact dates (*ah, I had that bad experience then*), but when we write in chronological order, they become more difficult to forget. It is important to reflect on the past, but the method of anchoring down the past in the form of a diary does not, try as one might, fit in with note-taking's concept of freeing one's mind and emotions.

Less so than carefully writing down the spread of ideas and pent-up feelings in your mind in a diary, it is easier to organize them writing out one sheet of Letter paper at a time. Rather than chronicling them, it's more like dynamically releasing them from your head, like writing them out of it.

There are three more reasons why I cannot recommend diaries. The first is that compared to Letter paper, they are far pricier. The second is that because they are shut closed, it is difficult to readily dash off some writing. And finally, in trying to make record of your thoughts then and there, you will likely go through a whole diary in two weeks, then sorting away the diary itself becomes a task. There's utterly no way to know where you wrote what.

There are notebooks which allow you to neatly tear out

each page, but I do not really recommend these either. Even if you tear them out at night before bed, it costs quite a bit of time. If you have that time, it is far better to use it to write a few more notes. Besides, if you are writing a large amount every day, before you know it you will need who knows how many notebooks, which adds up to a considerable sum of money.

I think many people take notes on their computer, using Word, PowerPoint, Excel, Keynote, and the like. However, on current computers, it is difficult to perform things like swiftly writing down your thoughts the moment they occur to you, quickly drawing up diagrams, organizing notes by laying them out, and sorting them into folders with other Letter documents and whatnot. From the get-go, it is impossible to write until you've booted up the computer. In the time that takes, whatever had floated into your mind will be long gone.

There are those for whom touch typing on a computer is far and away faster than writing by hand. While this aspect would certainly hold true if it were just words, trying to add even a simple diagram blows this notion out of the water. An illustration you could draw in ten seconds takes five or even ten minutes, halting your train of thought.

A resulting problem with computers is beginning to think you can only write in words. Things that would be effortless to express in a diagram, too, you will end up trying to express with only words. You will naturally end up truncating things that are difficult to express in words. It's the same with smartphones and tablets, too. It's impossible to quickly draw up things like a 2x2 framework, and with four to six lines totaling roughly seventy-five words in one minute, it is almost impossible to begin with. Naturally it is also impossible to rearrange notes to deepen your thoughts.

If digital paper becomes incredibly cheap, and it becomes possible to line up ten pages at one, and it becomes completely unnecessary to worry about power supply, and it becomes possible to write by hand in exactly the same way, and keyboards undergo drastic improvements as well—*then* there will be room for reconsideration. But for the time being, the feeling of invigoration born from steadily scrawling on paper, the new discoveries made by rearranging notes you've written, the sense of security achieved by swiftly organizing notes by throwing them into seven to ten folders—such things are the merits of paper, and at present it would be difficult to substitute with any other method.

Figuring out how to write notes anywhere within one minute

The optimal pen for note-taking

In order to finish writing each note within one minute, your choice of writing materials is crucial. Not being able to write fluidly will put you over the time limit. I recommend the "PILOT VBALL Recycled Rolling Ball Stick pen with Liquid Ink." It glides well without requiring any pressure. Moreover, the ink never blotches or fails to come out, allowing you to write clean to the end.

What I most highly recommend against are mechanical

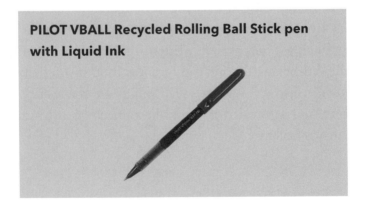

PILOT VBALL Recycled Rolling Ball Stick pen with Liquid Ink

pencils. I think that compared to the PILOT VBALL, writing speed likely drops more than twenty to thirty percent. Old types of ballpoint pens, too, require you to be aware of how hard you press down, making it both difficult to write fast and tiring to write many pages.

It seems a small thing to fuss over, but I believe that in order to continue writing ten or more pages every day, one's choice of writing materials is crucial. As I am always recommending this pen and frequently gifting it to others, after having taught note-taking to hundreds of people at a major consumer goods maker, I have even had the experience of the general affairs department purchasing a large quantity of them as "Akaba-san's pen."

Learning to write notes wherever you are

Since I began to write Letter notes, I constantly keep a hundred or so sheets of one-side-used Letter paper prepared in my desks both at the office and at home. I also keep twenty more in my attaché case. It's important that I be able to write instantaneously the moment an idea hits me, no matter where I am. It depends on the length of the trip, but when I have business trips overseas, I bring sixty to seventy pages along just in case. There is an extraordinary amount of stimuli during overseas business trips, so

I end up wanting to write many notes. I make a point of not failing to record in writing these precious realizations.

There are also many people who love using a clipboard like in the picture below. This is because it makes it possible to write on the spot, even if at a meeting somewhere in the office. This is of course the same in one's home as well. It is important to be able to write immediately from anywhere using one's individual preference.

When utilizing a clipboard, I recommend having the

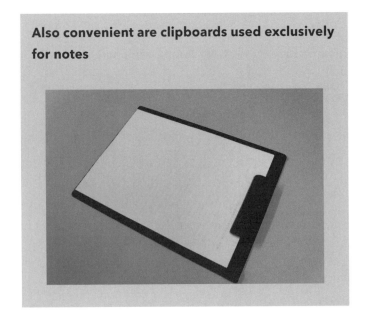

Also convenient are clipboards used exclusively for notes

clip on the right side. The reasons for this are that since the title and main text of notes is written from the left edge, doing so makes it easier to write, and also after turning over the page, the title will still be easy to read. Of course, you will properly sort your ten to fifteen written pages into folders every evening before bed.

Still, there will also be times when, like when on the train, you cannot spread out a sheet of Letter paper but want to write no matter what. To do so, fold your Letter

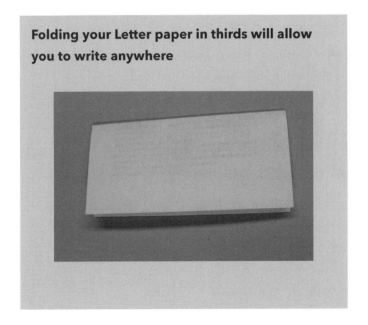

Folding your Letter paper in thirds will allow you to write anywhere

paper in thirds, then write normally on the top section. Since the width is then one-third, it will be narrow, but go on to write as usual. Men can put these in the chest pockets of their suits or shirts, and women can use their handbags.

The reasons behind going to such lengths to write are that if you don't write whatever down the moment you think of it, then it will disappear, and also that even in writing out clean drafts somewhere else, new ideas will steadily occur to you, which is why I place such emphasis on writing them down onto notes. Notes that you have written out like this can also be dealt with the same as other ones, and you will not have wasted any time at all.

Putting feelings into thoughts, and thoughts into notes

There are occasionally people who, even if they try to start note-taking, do not know what to write. The following diagram explains the circumstances and subsequent stages for such times.

From consolidating emotions into thoughts and putting them into notes until tackling issue resolution

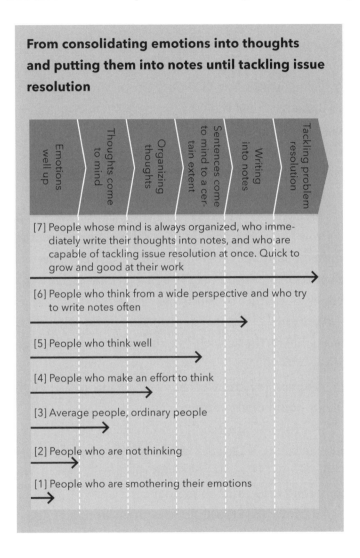

Emotions well up → Thoughts come to mind → Organizing thoughts → Sentences come to mind to a certain extent → Writing into notes → Tackling problem resolution

[7] People whose mind is always organized, who immediately write their thoughts into notes, and who are capable of tackling issue resolution at once. Quick to grow and good at their work

[6] People who think from a wide perspective and who try to write notes often

[5] People who think well

[4] People who make an effort to think

[3] Average people, ordinary people

[2] People who are not thinking

[1] People who are smothering their emotions

Everyone has emotions. Happy, sad, like, dislike, painful, want to do, don't want to do—the list goes on. Following feeling, some sort of thought comes to mind. When one organizes that thought, sentences come to mind to a certain extent. Write those sentences into notes. After writing them into notes, tackle some sort of issue resolution—such is the flow of it. However, everyone is at their own level, so that is what this graph compares.

At arrow [1] at the bottom are people who are smothering their emotions. If emotions are smothered, it becomes difficult for them to arise. It is not a state of having no feelings, but rather of concealing them.

At arrow [2] are people who are not thinking. Emotions come to the surface, but thoughts are hard-pressed to form.

At arrow [3] are average, ordinary people. Thoughts come to mind to a certain extent.

At arrow [4] are people who make an effort to think and who can to a certain extent organize their thoughts.

At arrow [5] are people who think well. To a certain extent sentences come to mind.

At arrow [6] are people who think from a wide perspective and who try to write notes often. Their thinking becomes considerably deep.

At arrow [7] are people whose mind is always organized, who immediately write their thoughts into notes, and who are capable of tackling issue resolution at once. They are quick to learn and capable of work. Those who are able to probe into this stage are capable of arriving at the "Zero Second Thinking" described in Chapter 2.

Dear reader: which stage are you at?

Examples of note titles by circumstance/needs

For note titles, it is best to immediately record down or write out what is leaving you feeling uneasy or whatever crosses your mind. Once you get used to this, you will become able to write out your feelings well, but in the beginning, there will be times you find yourself at a loss. For this, I tried writing out titles to serve as references for when you may get stuck. Even if you aren't stuck on a title, there might be one in here that strikes home for whatever situation you find yourself in. I've provisionally written in positions, names, and languages, so I certainly want for you to make those spots specific to you.

Quieting and organizing your mind

Finding composure
when you are upset at your boss

- Why did my section manager say that in such a nasty way?
- What did she think, saying it like that? That it's fine?
- What was her intention?
- Was it just that she was in a bad mood?
- What did everyone else think, seeing her be so curt?
- Who would she have spoken more politely with?
- In what kind of situations has she spoken more politely with me?
- If I were her, how would I have said it?
- What does she look like to our department head?
- How do my coworkers see her?

Cheering up a bit when you're feeling down

- When do I have a hard time cheering up?
- When do I feel cheerful?
- Have I always been this way?
- Who's always cheerful? How do they keep their spirits up?
- Who's always feeling down? Why is that?
- What does so-and-so, who's always down on themself, look like to others?

- What do I look like to others when I'm feeling downcast?
- What can I do to seem more cheerful?
- Can I fake it till I make it?
- Will I feel a little better if I let go of all my pent-up feelings?

Keeping your nerves under control

- Why is my heart beating so fast right now?
- When does my heart race?
- When do things end without my heart racing?
- What does it even mean when my heart beats fast?
- Who never seems to be fazed? Why is that?
- Would clarifying my anxieties make my heart settle down?
- What happens when my heart races?
- Did my heart not race that much before?
- Being calm and self-possessed—what is that state for me?
- Even if my heart races, is there a way to behave without minding?

To stop getting stage fright

- When do I get stage fright?
- When do I not get stage fright?
- Since when did I start getting stage fright?
- Who do I always get stage fright in front of?

- What qualities do people who don't get stage fright have?
- Why don't they get stage fright?
- For me to do the same as them and stop getting stage fright?
- Is stage fright simply from being overly self-conscious?
- What would happen if I were to think I don't mind even when I get stage fright?
- As long as I produce results, is it the same whether I get stage fright or not?

To stop being overly self-conscious

- When do I become overly self-conscious?
- What is the state of being overly self-conscious?
- What do I become overly self-conscious for?
- Who's overly self-conscious? What do they look like to others?
- What are overly self-conscious people thinking about?
- What would my overly self-conscious self look like if viewed objectively?
- Is being overly self-conscious the flip side of not being self-confident?
- Are being overly self-conscious and having a lot of pride mostly the same thing?
- What does it mean to have a lot of pride?
- What is having a lot of pride "a lot" in comparison to?

Getting rid of self-hatred

- Why do I hate myself?
- What the hell even is self-hatred?
- What originally set off my self-hatred?
- Is self-hatred the flip side of having unreasonable expectations?
- When do I hate myself?
- Who seems to not hate themself? Why is that?
- What do I feel after having an episode of self-hatred?
- What would I feel like if I didn't hate myself?
- Is self-hatred not just simply a form of babying one-self?
- For me, what would it look like to not hate myself every day?

Growing closer to others

- What can I do to get closer to others?
- What can I do to get closer to so-and-so?
- When am I able to get closer?
- When am I unable to become close?
- What does becoming closer with others mean to me?
- How do I feel when I'm unable to get closer with others?
- How do people who are able to get close with any-one behave?

- Is it never painful for them to get close with anyone?
- What values do they have that make it easy for them to get close with others?
- For behaving in a way that makes it easier to become close with anyone starting tomorrow?

To stop bad-mouthing others

- Who do I end up bad-mouthing?
- When do I end up bad-mouthing?
- How do I feel after bad-mouthing someone?
- Why am I unable to stop bad-mouthing people?
- Could it be that I bad-mouth people because I'm envious of them?
- When I bad-mouth others, what do I look like to those around me?
- When I don't bad-mouth others, what do I look like to those around me?
- How do people who don't bad-mouth others sort out their emotions?
- How can I avoid people who bad-mouth others?
- What *is* bad-mouthing in the first place?

Not minding even when others bad-mouth you

- For not minding even when others bad-mouth me?
- To not be agitated at all by being bad-mouthed, to

what extent do I need to be mentally disciplined?
- What kind of bad-mouthing am I not bothered by?
- When am I not bothered by being bad-mouthed?
- What kind of bad-mouthing is especially impermissible?
- Why is a certain type of bad-mouthing particularly upsetting?
- What do people who don't mind at all even if they are bad-mouthed do?
- How do they digest what is said about them?
- Does having self-confidence make you not mind being bad-mouthed?
- Does being bad-mouthed have to do with having good or bad luck?

Becoming someone who accepts help from others

- What can I do to allow myself to be helped when I need it?
- Is there not something I can do about my unwillingness to accept help at times when I need to seek it out?
- What does being helped by others mean to me?
- What attributes do those who are able to properly accept help have?
- What do I need to do to learn to be that way too?
- Why do I hate being helped by others this much?

- Have I ever had a problem after being helped an appropriate amount?
- What if I don't accept help when I need it and then things get worse—then what?
- Why do people try to help me?
- Could it be that I'm allergic to people who let themselves be spoiled?

To stop excessively depending on others

- When do I depend on others too much?
- What does it mean to be overly dependent?
- Since when did I start being overly dependent?
- Is it unattractive to be overly dependent?
- How do I feel after being overly dependent?
- How does whoever I was depending on feel?
- Why do they let me be overly dependent on them?
- What do those who aren't overly dependent on others do?
- What is an appropriate level of dependence?
- For being appropriately dependent next time?

To stop feeling isolated

- When do I feel isolated?
- Why do I feel this isolated?
- When I feel isolated, how should I cope with it?

- What kind of people don't feel isolated?
- Why are people who don't feel isolated capable of doing so?
- Could it be that my feelings of isolation are just a figment of my imagination?
- Could my feelings of isolation be some kind of masochism?
- How can I learn to live well with my feelings of isolation?
- If I socialized more would I feel less isolated?
- What kind of socializing would make me feel less isolated?

Being emotionally self-reliant

- For being emotionally self-reliant?
- When do I feel like I'm able to be self-reliant?
- Why do I quickly resort to depending on others?
- Who always seems to be self-reliant?
- Is it possible that they always appear self-reliant but in reality are quite dependent?
- If I become able to do anything by myself, could I then say that I'm self-reliant?
- Why is it that I always want to lean on something?
- What does being self-reliant mean to me?
- For me, would being self-reliant mean leaving my parents' house?

- For being emotionally independent even if I'm still somewhat financially reliant on them?

Becoming able to love one's parents

- What can I do to become able to love my parents?
- How can I love my parents after they've done such horrible things?
- Why on earth did they continue doing such horrible things to me?
- Lately my parents are turning to me for help in one way or another, but I absolutely cannot forgive them. What should I do?
- They suddenly drop by whenever they're sick or feeling faint-hearted—how can I care for parents like that?
- What can I do to be able to see the good in them?
- What do people who don't particularly struggle to love their parents feel?
- Do all kids who were raised normally carry a deep affection for their parents?
- What about kids from non-normal homes, what the heck can they do?
- When will I become able to forgive my parents?

Becoming self-confident

- What can I do to be more self-confident?

- When do I not have self-confidence?
- Who always has self-confidence? Why are they able to feel that way?
- What kind of effect do self-confident people have on those around them?
- What kind of impression do self-confident people leave?
- What does it mean to have self-confidence?
- Do I in fact have self-confidence? Or maybe not?
- For making sure that I feel self-confidence later on?
- For producing results even when I'm not confident in myself?
- For making sure I don't think much about whether or not I'm confident in myself?

Being able to organize one's mind

- When am I able to organize my mind?
- Regarding what topics am I able to organize my mind well?
- What's good about having my mind organized?
- Why am I in trouble when I can't organize my mind?
- What do I not mind being mentally unorganized about?
- Who always has their mind organized? How do they do so?
- What do people who always have their minds organized look like?

- What do people who are mentally unorganized look like to others?
- What's the relationship between being able to organize one's mind and being smart?
- What's the relationship between being able to organize one's mind and emotional things?

Communicating smoothly

Smoothly carrying out communication over email with one's boyfriend

- Why doesn't he reply to me right away?
- When does he promptly reply to me?
- Does emailing become bothersome after you've been dating for a while?
- Could it be that he doesn't really like using email, even though he has no problem with phone calls?
- Is he bad about emails at work too?
- What if we decided on a time to email each other?
- Is he reluctant to send emails to other people too?
- In order to not get irritated by his emails?
- Maybe he doesn't really like long emails?
- Would it be better to not really exchange emails with him?

Making communication with one's boss easier

- What style of communication does my department head prefer?
- What style of communication does he especially dislike?
- When is he in a good mood?
- When is he in an especially bad mood?
- For communicating well with him, regardless of his mood?
- Who's able to communicate well with him? How do they do it?
- What's his work style? What would be a communication style that harmonizes with it?
- What is he good at?
- What is he bad at?
- What kind of communication does he use with his own higher-ups?

Making communication with one's subordinates easier

- What do I need to be careful about when communicating with my subordinates?
- What exactly did I do during times I was able to communicate with my subordinates well?
- What went wrong during times I wasn't able to communicate with my subordinates well?

- What image do my subordinates have of me?
- What expectations do my subordinates have of me?
- What is the ideal boss for subordinates?
- How should I behave towards my subordinates?
- How should I behave towards female subordinates?
- How should I behave towards male subordinates?
- How do my co-workers behave towards our subordinates?

Becoming able to speak with anyone

- What can I do to become able to speak with anyone without being timid?
- Who do I have no problem speaking with?
- What's my mood like after speaking with no problem?
- What's my mood like after having been unable to speak well?
- Who's unable to speak well?
- Who's able to speak well with anyone without any problems? Why are they able to do that?
- What about such people can I likely imitate?
- What would people think if my attitude were to change depending on who I'm speaking to?
- What in the world does it mean for my attitude to change?
- I almost certainly didn't have problems in elementary

school. What can I do to be like that again?

Becoming less reserved with others

- Why do I end up being so reserved with others even when it's about me?
- When do I end up being reserved?
- Can I obtain high evaluations by being reserved?
- Who am I reserved towards?
- Toward whom do I not feel the need to be so reserved?
- What's awkward when I'm excessively reserved with others?
- Who isn't reserved towards other people? Does that cause any problems for them?
- Since when did I become this reserved? What was the cause?
- If you don't have self-confidence does it make you reserved?
- Could being reserved be a form of escapism?

Accomplishing your goals

Making up one's mind and following through without getting frustrated

- For carrying out my decisions without getting frustrated?
- Who's able to carry out their decisions without getting frustrated? How do they do so?
- Do they have a certain way of thinking or approach that allows them to not get frustrated?
- What *is* frustration in the first place?
- Will I feel more at ease if I start thinking it's fine to get frustrated?
- If I truly set my heart on whatever then will it be difficult to get frustrated?
- What way of deciding or charging ahead makes it difficult to get frustrated?
- What has been my biggest frustration so far? How did my life change because of it?
- What's the difference between what is frustrating and what isn't?
- If I decide on something, how about I just try it out without thinking hard on it?

Continuing with one's foreign language studies without getting frustrated

- For being sure this time to study Spanish thoroughly?
- In order to not get frustrated in my Spanish studies?
- With studying Spanish, why am I passionate only in the beginning?
- For making studying Spanish more interesting?
- When am I able to continue smoothly with my Spanish studies?
- Would it be good to test out somewhere what I've learned from studying Spanish?
- For making foreign friends?
- What if I tried making foreign friends on Facebook and corresponded on there?
- What do I need to speak about in Spanish when I'm on business trips?
- What if I tried listing out all of the greeting phrases and explanatory sentences I need to be able to say in Spanish and practiced them?

Organizing one's vision for the future

- After one year, what do I want to do?
- After one year, what situation would make me satisfied?
- After three years, what kind of person do I want to become?

- My vision for three years ahead?
- After three years, what situation would make me satisfied?
- To that end, where do I need to be within six months from now?
- To make my vision a reality, what are the things I want to master no matter what?
- What are my strong points?
- With whom and how should I consult about my vision?
- What does having a vision even mean in the first place?

Deciding on one's future education

- Is it necessary to go to university?
- What would be the merits of continuing on to university?
- What would be the demerits of continuing on to university?
- Would university be interesting?
- If I went to university even though I don't really want to study, would I not regret it?
- Is there a way to know the vibe of a campus beforehand?
- What does everyone do at university?
- I know a lot of people ahead of me in school who are immersed in their part-time jobs, but is that good enough?

- What if I went to a vocational school?
- What if I went to a vocational school and focused on the subjects I like?

Deciding on a place of employment

- Should I take a job with this company?
- What are the merits of taking a job with this company?
- What are the demerits of taking a job with this company?
- To begin with, what do I want to do most in my work?
- In order to not have a salary be my only objective?
- Should I ask some of my older friends?
- What does getting a job mean to me?
- If I start at a company, what will be most different from up until now?
- Graduates who wait a year or two before starting work are increasing, but what will I do?
- Will I be fine at this company?

Changing jobs

- What jobs suit me?
- Can I achieve self-actualization at my current company?
- Would changing jobs solve everything?
- In changing jobs, what do I need to prepare?
- Regarding changing jobs, to whom do I need to ask what?
- The risks of changing jobs?

- If I change jobs, where do I need to go?
- What would happen if I changed jobs?
- What stories might my older friends who have changed jobs have?
- They say if you change jobs once then you'll change them again and again, but what's that about?

Studying abroad

- Should I study abroad or not?
- If I were to study abroad, when and where should I go?
- Am I capable of learning enough Spanish to get by abroad?
- What's the purpose of studying abroad?
- How would it be if I were to not study abroad?
- What would I be able to achieve by studying abroad?
- The risks of studying abroad?
- What do I need to prepare starting now?
- How should I look up information about studying abroad?
- How to prepare for study abroad expenses?

Getting married}

- Should I marry this person?
- What would happen if I didn't marry this person?
- The risks of marriage?

- The merits of marriage?
- Is everyone happy after getting married?
- Cases where someone was unhappy after getting married?
- What does marriage even mean to me?
- In order to be happy after getting married?
- What are the difficult parts of marriage?
- Why does everyone get married?

Making one's private life a priority

- What can I do to become able to make my private life more of a priority?
- How to distinguish between my private life and my work life?
- How do people who do a good job of prioritizing their private life do so?
- What happens to people who can't do a good job of keeping their private life separate?
- For being able to work well while also making my private life a priority?
- If I don't make my private life a priority, will I also be unable to get work done?
- What is a private life in the first place?
- People who do what they love for work are all immersed in it, but what's that about?

- If you love your work and that can't be helped, then what should you do?
- For dating someone who doesn't understand that your work is fun for you?

Growing and becoming able to work better

Being able to grow quickly
- When am I able to grow quickly?
- When can I actually feel that I'm growing quickly?
- Around when was I growing quickly?
- When I'm able to grow quickly, what does the world look like?
- When I'm able to grow quickly, what do the people around me look like?
- What does being able to grow quickly look like to me?
- When is it difficult to grow quickly?
- When it's difficult to grow quickly, what's not going well?
- For me, what environment makes it impossible to grow quickly?
- For changing an environment that makes it hard to grow quickly?

Becoming good at one's work
- What pressure points do people who are good at

their work have pinned down?

- Why is so-and-so good at their work?
- Why did so-and-so stop being a good worker?
- When do I actually feel that I've gotten good at my work?
- What does being good at work mean to me?
- In order to get better at my work, how should I put in the effort?
- What's the bottleneck I hit in striving to speed up my pace at work?
- How to strike a balance between speed and quality in my work?
- How do people who are good at their work successfully juggle speed and quality?
- How can I make being good at my work and a kindness towards others coexist?

Becoming able to produce proposal ideas

- When do proposal ideas come to me continuously?
- Times I've been in trouble when proposal ideas came to me one after another?
- Points for producing proposal ideas one after another?
- In order to produce proposal ideas, what kind of information gathering is necessary?
- In order to consolidate gathered information into proposal ideas?

- For producing proposal ideas, what do I need to focus my attention on?
- What traits do those who produce proposal ideas one after another have?
- Are people who produce proposal ideas one after another picky about the quality of each idea?
- Is my reason for being unable to produce proposal ideas *not* just mere hesitation?
- Could my reason for being unable to produce proposal ideas be that I think I'm incapable of doing so?

Becoming able to write proposals

- How to pour proposal ideas into a table of contents?
- How to think up a proposal's organization?
- What if I created three or so patterns for proposal organization?
- Facets of those who compose proposals quickly?
- When and how do people who compose proposals quickly write them?
- What were the circumstances like at times when I was able to write a proposal well?
- Would spending time on proposals help me write good ones?
- How to prepare proposal illustrations and charts?
- After writing a proposal, how to then finalize it?

- Are being able to write proposals well and the quality of the proposal content itself interrelated?

Raising one's antenna

- What does it mean to raise one's antenna?
- What must I do to raise my antenna?
- Is it possible to always keep my antenna raised?
- When and regarding what themes do I have my antenna raised?
- People who are good at keeping their antennas raised?
- How does so-and-so always keep their antenna raised that much?
- What's the relationship between having a raised antenna and one's ability to gather information?
- For keeping my antenna raised even when I'm low on time?
- What's the relationship between raising one's antenna and being good at one's work?
- Could it be that sending out one's own signal is also necessary for raising one's antenna?

Not being negligent in gathering information

- What must I do to not be negligent in gathering information?
- How do people who are always gathering information do so?

- How much time do people who are capable of gathering information spend on it?
- Do those who are good at their work have some kind of trick for information gathering as well?
- With what system should I move forward in gathering information?
- How to make proper use of both online information and information gained in person?
- In order to not spend an excessive amount of time on gathering information?
- For constantly checking the appropriateness of my information gathering methods?
- What if I limited my exposure to online information to three times a day—morning, midday, and evening—at fifteen minutes each?
- For radically elevating the quality of my information gathering?

Staying highly attuned
- For constantly staying highly attuned?
- What does it mean to be highly attuned?
- What kind of efforts do those who are highly attuned make?
- When do I feel like I am not highly attuned?
- What do people think when they look at people who

are *not* highly attuned?

- What do people think when they look at people who *are* highly attuned?
- Would continuing with gathering information make me highly attuned?
- For moving ahead to become even more highly attuned?
- How should I go about searching for highly attuned people?
- For constantly surrounding myself with highly attuned people?

Enriching one's sensibility

- What is sensibility?
- What determines the way people feel?
- Who has a rich sensibility? Why is it rich?
- Why is so-and-so said to have a rich sensibility?
- Why is so-and-so said to have an overly particular sensibility?
- Who does not have a rich sensibility? Why is that? What's different with them?
- How to polish my sensibility?
- Am I capable of polishing my sensibility?
- Can I truly not do a good job of explaining my sensibility in words?

- With my sensibility, is it just that I skip out on explaining it in words?

Being able to speak well in meetings

- For speaking well in meetings?
- When am I able to speak well in meetings?
- When have I not been able to speak well in meetings?
- How to recover when I'm unable to speak well?
- Who's remarks at meetings go over well?
  What's their trick?
- Who's remarks at meetings don't go over well? Why does that end up being the case?
- What should be done to prepare for meetings?
- For properly listening to others' remarks at meetings then speaking well myself?
- Pointers for having meetings proceed well?
- How to contribute to meetings?

Becoming better at giving presentations

- How to carry out practice for giving presentations?
- How much practice will it take to feel confident in giving presentations?
- How to do a good job of organizing the spoken content and written content of presentations?
- What kind of preparation do those who are good at

giving presentations do?

- What ways of thinking and of captivating others do those who are good at giving presentations employ?
- What does a presentation look like when done well?
- What does a presentation look like when done poorly?
- For giving an effective presentation?
- For getting told that my presentations have gotten better?
- Tricks for not getting stage fright when giving presentations?

At this we have 400 titles. Delving deep into and writing from different angles on each title will easily yield close to a thousand pages of notes. For those who want to grow in a short period of time, and those who want to stop fretting constantly, by all means I want for you to try writing these out.

If something floats to your mind, it is good if you can write it down right away. In times when your mind is clouded, too, I want for you to simply clear it out without trying to write well. At times when no matter what nothing comes to mind, or while you are still not accustomed to note-taking, it is fine to use the 400 titles listed above.

Since there is no labor required to think of titles, this

can likely be done in two to three weeks' time. Having undergone this, without a doubt your mind will become organized, and you will become someone who rarely loses their composure.

Chapter 4

Utilizing Notes
to the Fullest Extent

Delving deep to make notes even more effective

With some notes, if you take the four to six lines you've written on one page, turn each one into a title, then write four to six more lines under those titles, your ideas will substantially deepen and become organized. The content will become one, two tiers richer, making you feel all the more refreshed.

Note 10

Why doesn't my department head talk to me?

12-1-2013

–Could it be that he wasn't pleased with my remarks at the meeting the other day?
–Could he be upset about the friction between me
  and the other section managers?
–It seems like he and his wife are always fighting,
  too–is he simply in a bad mood?
–Is it not just that he's busy and simply doesn't
  have time to talk to me?

For example, suppose you've written Note 10— "Why doesn't my department head talk to me?"

In this case, you would take the following lines of main text—

> "Could it be that he wasn't pleased with my remarks at the meeting the other day?""Could he be upset about the friction between me and the other section managers?"
>
> "It seems like he and his wife are always fighting, too— is he simply in a bad mood?"
>
> "Is it not just that he's busy and simply doesn't have time to talk to me?"

—and turn each one into the title of a new note.

To start with, line one— "Could it be that he wasn't pleased with my remarks at the meeting the other day?"— would become Note 11.

Herewith, the phrase "Could it be that my department head wasn't pleased with my remarks," which incidentally

Note 11

Could it be that my department head wasn't pleased with my remarks at the meeting the other day?   **12-1-2013**

–Did I object too much to my department head's proposition at the meeting the other day?
–Certainly there's no problem with the content of what I said, so was it the way I said it?
–Is it even possible for me to make remarks he'll be pleased with?
–I'll try out making my own remarks a little more considerate of the intent behind his remarks

---

occurred to you, deepens in the following way, where the points at issue are analyzable, even ending in introspection:

–Did I object too much to my department head's proposition at the meeting the other day?
–Certainly there's no problem with the content of what I said, so was it the way I said it?
–Is it even possible for me to make remarks he'll be pleased with?

Note 12

Could my department head be upset about the friction between me and the other section managers?   **12-1-2013**

–He seemed to be upset over the arguing at the section manager meeting the other day

–Could he have heard my clash with Kaneda afterwards?

–But he didn't seem to take notice of the friction among other section managers

–He was upset the next day, but since then he seems to have forgotten about it

---

–I'll try out making my own remarks a little more considerate of the intent behind his remarks

This would be the same for the second and subsequent lines.

In Note 12, after writing out your anxieties regarding whether the department head is upset over the friction between you and another section manager, you reach the judgement that it ultimately seems fine to not be concerned. By writing in this way, you will put an end to

Note 13

> **It seems my department head and his wife**
> **are always fighting, too—is he simply in a bad**
> **mood?**   **12-1-2013**
>
> —Generally, my department head is in a bad mood
>   on Mondays
> —When he's in a bad mood, anything you say is futile
> —If it's just that he's in a bad mood, then no worry-
>   ing on my part will change that
> —Let's try ignoring it today

dragging around what's been weighing you down. You will see that it's fine to not become preoccupied with superfluous matters.

The third line would turn into a note like Note 13.

By considering that your department head may simply be in a bad mood, meaning no need to be concerned, you settle on the conclusion that it is good to not read so much into things. This alone considerably reduces the burden on your mind.

Note 14

> **Is it not just that my department head's busy**
> **and simply doesn't have time to talk to me?**
>
> **12-1-2013**
>
> —With the proposal for the day after tomorrow not
>   yet in order, things are hectic for him
> —Even at the best of times, he's busy and really
>   doesn't seem to have time to speak with subor-
>   dinates
> —I'm surely no special case

And finally, line four becomes Note 14.

By writing this, it becomes clear that less so than being in a bad mood, your department head might just be busy, and thus your concerns might be groundless.

Even if your coworkers tell you you're overthinking it, your mood might not readily clear up; however, by writing in this way, you will come to not worry needlessly.

In other words, just by writing these four pages, you are able to delve deep into the original note which flashed to your mind, and to far and away more correctly compre-

Note 15

How to be sure this year to become able to speak English without getting frustrated?

12-1-2013

–Why do I never keep at it very long?

–Why is it that I don't see results even during stretches of 3 to 4 weeks of enthusiastic study?

–Would it be good to find someone highly motivated who I can study together with?

–Should I be making more practical use of the TOEIC exam?

hend your department head's feelings and the position in which you have been placed in. You will feel more at ease, and your work will progress more smoothly.

Once again, supposing that you've written a note titled "How to be sure this year to become able to speak English without getting frustrated?" it might look like Note 15.

Though you might be experiencing frustration that your English studies are not progressing along, *how* you should

Note 16

> ### Why don't I keep at my English studies for long?
> **12-1-2013**
>
> —After a short time, I get distracted by something
>   else and become absorbed in it
> —Since I can't really see results, my motivation goes
>   away
> —Is it that the way I study is monotonous, that I
>   scarcely change things up?
> —Until now, what have I stuck with before?

make improvements surfaces to some extent in lines three and four.

Thereupon, you might try writing a fresh note in relation to the first line, as with Note 16.

The reason for being unable to keep at it very long is becoming considerably clearer. What is becoming visible through these additional notes is not only the reason for being unable to keep at it, but also hints as to what

Note 17

Why is it that I don't see results in my English even during stretches of three to four weeks of enthusiastic study? 12-1-2013

—Am I not producing results? Or can I simply not see them?

—What can I do to be able to sense results?

—What if I changed my plan of attack and studied in a way that makes results easier to see?

—Is there a way to not lose my motivation even if I don't see results?

might help you do so—that you're preoccupied with other things, that your motivation disappears because you can't see results, that the way you study might be monotonous, or consideration as to what change of perspective would help you keep at it, and so on.

Line two from Note 15 turns into Note 17.

Regarding the single word "results," this note is getting at the core of whether you really aren't producing them, or whether you simply cannot see them, and how

Note 18

Would it be good to find someone highly motivated who I can study together with?

12-1-2013

—It would be good if I could study together with highly motivated people who don't get disheartened

—Where could I find someone?

—What are the merits of a study partner?

—Would a rival be good? Or someone I can keep up with?

to best sense them. Furthermore, by probing into how to change your plan of attack such that results are easier to see, or into whether there's a way to not lose your motivation even if you don't see results, you are able to change your mind in a considerably creative way.

Line three is turned into the title of Note 18.

Regarding the solution-strategy-oriented sentence "Would it be good to find someone highly motivated who I can study together with?" we have floating to the sur-

Note 19

Should I be making more practical use of the TOEIC exam? 12-1-2013

—By taking the TOEIC exam, I could work in more variety

—How would it be if I took it every time?

—Do TOEIC exam scores and studying English correspond to each other?

—Apart from the TOEIC, what else should I do?

---

face even more incisive answers, or perhaps sentences that hint at answers, such as "It would be good if I could study together with highly motivated people who don't get disheartened," or "Would a rival be good? Or someone I can keep up with?" and so on.

A note relating to line four becomes Note 19.

"By taking the TOEIC exam, I could work in more variety," "Do TOEIC exam scores and studying English correspond to each other?" "Apart from the TOEIC, what else should I do?"—such thoughts break one step forward into new solution strategies.

In this way, if you write notes then turn the four to six lines of main text into titles, writing out new notes in succession, your ideas will immediately deepen. I recommend this because, although you will use a lot of paper, your mind will become more and more organized each time you write. Others will likely take notice of how astonishingly quick your thinking has become. As you delve deeper, you will go on to hit upon new ideas one after another. Once this becomes so, the feeling that you are wasting paper will vanish. You will come to see various new things, fresh ideas will follow in succession, and anything and everything will come to be enjoyable.

It is also fine to delve deeper into the main text of notes written while delving deep (the last example of such a note being the one titled "Should I be making more practical use of the TOEIC exam?"). In this case, turn the main text into titles— "By taking the TOEIC exam, I could work in more variety," "How would it be if I took it every time?" "Do TOEIC exam scores and studying English correspond to each other?" "Apart from the TOEIC, what else should I do?"—and go on to write notes using them.

In using this method of basing four to six more pages of notes off of a single-page note, if you can think up just one title, then you can continue writing in succession without any worries.

When you delve deep into one title (or theme), you can expect the sizeable payoff of difficult problems being subdivided, dismantled, and sortable while you come to understand the broader picture, all in the blink of an eye.

Writing on the same theme from different angles

In addition to delving deep, towards a single important theme, if you write not just one page *but many* from various angles, your outlook will greatly broaden. As such, I recommend doing so. Your mind will be better organized, and you will become capable of making considerably composed judgements even regarding emotional matters.

For example, suppose you have written the following note:

"Why do I lose my motivation so quickly?"

- –I always quickly get frustrated, even when I resolve on something
- –Back when I was a teenager I never had this prob-

lem—since when did that change?
—I'm always able to read books, and I never get frustrated
—Pretty soon, I'll have to be able to continue with my resolutions. As it stands is no good

The method is to from there write notes with titles like the following:

- When do I stay motivated?
- When in particular does my motivation run out?
- Towards what do I stay motivated?
- How do people who are always motivated maintain it?
- How do motivated people cope with negative emotions?
- Do those people never get frustrated?
- Could I not copy how motivated people do things?
- What even is motivation in the first place? Is it perseverance?
- Is it bad to just do things that are fun, or that I feel are worth doing?

If done in this way, after the ten or so minutes it takes to finish writing those notes, your mind will be considerably refreshed. *When do you feel motivated and capable of continuing on? When are you liable to get frustrated?* You will come to see ever so slightly the workings of your heart.

Again, for example, suppose you've written the following note:

"Why doesn't he share important information about work with me!?"

—Does he hate sharing information to begin with? Things like this have occasionally happened before

—Does he not share information because it's a pain in the ass? He's also lazy as hell

—Is it that he doesn't think of me often, so it's only me he doesn't share information with?

—Or, is it merely a matter of feeling motivated? When he's feeling motivated, he contacts me quite a bit

Afterwards, write notes with titles like the following ones:

• When does he share information with me?
• Who does he share information with?
• Regarding work, does he understand what is and isn't important?
• When he doesn't share information, what's he feeling like?

- Who properly shares information with everyone? Why are they able to do so?
- Conversely, am I properly sharing information?
- Maybe he thinks that, in the same way, I don't share information as well?
- When do people voluntarily share information with me?

If done in this way, *why* he doesn't share information and *when* he does will become quite apparent. What started as the one-sided dissatisfaction embodied in *why doesn't he share important information about work with me!?* will be considerably reduced by understanding the reason behind his incapability to adequately share information. At the very least, you will move one or two steps forward towards solving the problem.

All people judge what's good and evil, what they like and dislike, from their own point of view. Understandably, one is not very aware whether theirs is biased or not. Consequently, this becomes a large source of stress as we clash with other people and fail to understand their behaviors.

In writing notes from different angles, you are able to put yourself in the shoes of others, which allows you to comprehend their viewpoints and behaviors more easily than before writing out the reasons behind them. As a matter of course, you will lose your anger. One-sided instances of you not feeling well will be a thing of the past.

Let's check out a different example. Suppose you have written the title "Why am I not able to assert what I think is wrong without hesitating?" In this scenario, in addition to your original note, write out more with titles like the following:

- •When am I unable to assert myself without hesitating?
- • What's unpleasant when I'm unable to assert myself without hesitating?
- • What would others think if I didn't hesitate to assert myself with them?
- • What do others think of the fact that I hesitate to assert myself?
- • Is the fact that I hesitate to assert myself because I don't know, concretely, what I should address?
- • What do I need to assert myself about with so-and-so? (Concretely, with four to five people)
- • Good circumstances and bad circumstances in which to assert myself without hesitating?

Doing so will help you understand the previously shackled true reasons behind your own feelings and actions more than ever before.

In this way, with things you believe are important, things about which you are becoming emotional, things that you have not finished digesting—writing on them from different angles possesses the following great merits:

- You will be able to see clearly new dimensions which until now you could not
- You will be able to fully consider that which you had not given adequate consideration to previously
- Behavior of others you thought to be impossible to decipher, behavior of others and of your own you thought to be absolutely awful—towards these, your comprehension will deepen; you will be able to take on new viewpoints
- Overall, you will be able to set straight your feelings of unease, and you will be able to take initiative as a new version of yourself

Writing over fifteen to twenty pages until you feel convinced

Whether you are delving deeper, or whether you are aiming to write from different angles, when you feel up to it, it is good to steadily continue writing without limiting yourself to ten pages per day.

Especially when you've had a bad experience, when you can't understand something no matter how hard you try, when something outrageous has you seething, when you're feeling dejected—whether you are delving deeper, or whether you are aiming to write from different angles, spending twenty minutes or so purging these feelings onto notes will leave you feeling wonderfully refreshed. Continue writing until you feel convinced.

Even if you find the other party to be unreasonable with no room for debate, as you go on to write notes, you will become able to think with a little more composure. Even if just a small amount, you might come to see the reasons behind their standpoint and behavior.

Even in cases where you are indignant that your high expectations for someone were betrayed, when you come to see *why* your expectations were high, *whether* they tried to meet those expectations, and *whether* they failed after trying to do so, you will grow able to consider the situation from a slightly different point of view.

Even in times when your mind is foggy and you feel uneasy because you're unable to express yourself, in purging yourself of that fog to reveal what was behind it, your mood will remarkably change. When you don't know what was behind it, you're liable to think in worse and worse directions. However, by understanding its true nature, you can grow able to think constructively, saying to yourself along the way *even at worst I can settle for this* or *no, I can manage this somehow or other.* Naturally, your feelings will settle as well.

Once you're able to write each page within one minute, getting to this point takes only fifteen to twenty minutes.

The model for further developing notes

Up to this point, I have introduced a style of note-taking on horizontal Letter paper with four to six lines per note. While this remains the fundamental model, as the successor model for once one has mastered note-taking, I recommend the following method of dividing your page between right and left then writing subtitles. For an example, see Note 20, which is divided between "Efforts so far" and "Hereafter."

Here's a separate set of possible subtitles:

- "Current issues" and "Countermeasures"
- "Phenomenon, symptoms" and "Essential issue"
- "Rival companies' approach" and "This company's

efforts"
- "Strengths" and "Weaknesses"
- "Plan 1" and "Plan 2"
- "Head office's efforts" and "Branch office's efforts"
- "Role of supervisors" and "Role of subordinates"

In any case, think of the most suitable options to match each title. Once you complete several hundred pages of note-taking, you will be capable of this subdividing method as well. Of course, when writing a note divided between left and right, two minutes will become necessary to write one page.

The relationship between notes and logic trees

What is known as a *logic tree* is the organization of the relationships between words into a tree structure. This and notes produced by delving deep are in fact the same thing.

In a logic tree, the offspring of A are A-1, A-2, A-3, and A-4; the offspring of A-1 are A-1-1, A-1-2, A-1-3, and A-1-4. This scenario is represented in the diagram on the next page.

Note 20

In order to be able to speak English   12-1-2013

Efforts so far
—Tried waking up 30 minutes earlier to study English, but in the end most days I couldn't wake up
—Enrolled in an English conversation school but most nights had to work overtime and couldn't go
—Bought DVDs thinking I would watch TV dramas in English, but still have only watched 3 times
—Booked an English lesson over Skype, but didn't continue with that since it was awkward and bothersome

Hereafter
—Since mornings are futile after all, I'll be sure to study 30-45 minutes after coming home at night
—Since participating in an English conversation school on weekdays is impossible, I'll look for a school for Saturday or Sunday
—Since watching TV dramas in English seems to be the most important after all, no matter what it takes watch 1 episode per day. 2 episodes per weekend day
—Take the TOEIC exam every time for incentive

In the case of notes produced by delving deep, the initial A corresponds to the title; A-1, A-2, A-3, and A-4 correspond to the lines of main text. A-1 corresponds to the title of the next page, and A-1-1, A-1-2, A-1-3, and A-1-4 correspond to the lines of main text of that page.

As you will understand by looking at the diagram, the

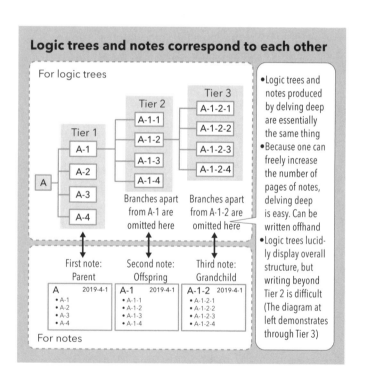

Logic trees and notes correspond to each other

For logic trees

Tier 1
A-1
A-2
A-3
A-4

Tier 2
A-1-1
A-1-2
A-1-3
A-1-4

Branches apart from A-1 are omitted here

Tier 3
A-1-2-1
A-1-2-2
A-1-2-3
A-1-2-4

Branches apart from A-1-2 are omitted here

A

First note:
Parent

A	2019-4-1
• A-1	
• A-2	
• A-3	
• A-4	

Second note:
Offspring

A-1	2019-4-1
• A-1-1	
• A-1-2	
• A-1-3	
• A-1-4	

Third note:
Grandchild

A-1-2	2019-4-1
• A-1-2-1	
• A-1-2-2	
• A-1-2-3	
• A-1-2-4	

For notes

- Logic trees and notes produced by delving deep are essentially the same thing
- Because one can freely increase the number of pages of notes, delving deep is easy. Can be written offhand
- Logic trees lucidly display overall structure, but writing beyond Tier 2 is difficult (The diagram at left demonstrates through Tier 3)

hierarchical relations cleanly correspond with each other.

The difference between the two is that with notes, one is able to single-mindedly write down whatever comes to mind *without* paying any heed to structure and the like. Then afterwards, upon arranging them, they naturally organize themselves into a logic tree-like formation.

Organizing ideas into a tree structure from scratch is not an easy thing to do, and it frequently costs time. It is also a stressful task, and catching sight of the broader picture is difficult while one is just beginning.

With notes, this concern is completely nonexistent. Just by writing one page per minute, the structure will naturally come into view.

Consolidating notes into proposals

Drawing up proposals is a burden. You think you'll write that, you think you'll write this, things you'd like to write rise to the surface and disappear, rise and disappear, and the proposal does not take shape.

It's common to not have enough material to write down, and it's also common to not have confidence in your ideas themselves. No one teaches you how to gather materials for writing, or what you can do to produce ideas you can feel somewhat confident in. It's lucky if you do have someone around who will teach you, but obtaining advice that cuts to the right points is a rare thing. I think it unfortunate that everyone figures out how to get along with just what they learn from imitating others.

There are a large number of books written on tips for writing proposals. However, even using them as a reference will not readily help you learn to write good proposals. Those who can glide through writing them are rare, and the majority of people scrape together several pages while grumbling to themselves. It's likely the norm for confidence to not scale with time spent, and to have the proposal you've gone to all that trouble to write nitpicked by your higher-ups.

Even so, once you have grown used to the note-taking method recommended in this book, you will be able to draft the skeletons of proposals in around thirty minutes. Writing fluidly, you will be able to conjure up an image for each proposal without stress. Once the skeleton and image are there, fleshing it out is relatively simple. Compared to before, the once confounding task of creating proposals and plans will be far easier. From here on, I'd like to speak to that process step by step.

Jotting down ideas one after another

First of all, whether it's this idea or that idea, write down one after another any idea that crosses your mind, using one page per idea. One page per idea means writing on a different page for each theme (or title).

It's fine to write a title then four to six lines on thoughts that come to flash into your mind, and it's also fine for the time being to just write a title. In that case, one page will not take one minute. Ten, twenty, or thirty seconds is enough to write it.

For example, supposing that by next week you must think up a plan for a new overseas tour geared towards those dissatisfied with the existing overseas tour, your title might look something like the following:

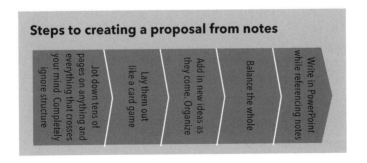

Steps to creating a proposal from notes

Jot down tens of pages on anything and everything that crosses your mind. Completely ignore structure

Lay them out like a card game

Add in new ideas as they come. Organize

Balance the whole

Write in PowerPoint while referencing notes

- Proposal to assemble desired destinations rather than a cookie-cutter selection
- Proposal to add in on-site itinerary flexibility
- Proposal to shift from being destination-focused to going with other excited travelers
- Proposal for specializing in gourmet tours rather than sightseeing
- Proposal for specializing in cheap and delicious local culinary tours rather than sightseeing
- Local home cooking tour
- Befriending like-minded locals tour
- Popular film actors' birthplace regional tour
- Coed 20-person help-build-elementary-school-buildings-in-Myanmar tour
- Explore the roots of Japanese culture in Taiwan tour

Or, if it were a proposal for a new English education in which anyone can become able to speak English:

- Training one's ear to hear intonation patterns in English
- Conduct listening competitions like games
- Enhance listening skills over a short time through tutorials focused on the characteristics of sounds in English
- Thoroughly read the same 50 essential sentences out

loud repeatedly
- The exercise frequency is automatically displayed and rankings appear
- Read articles in English in fields one is interested in
- Among online English articles, distribute only articles in fields of interest in big font
- As soon as something is read aloud in a big voice it is scored. Results are ranked
- Compete in real time to read out loud the same composition online
- Teach over a short, focused period a method of intonation and pronunciation that creates the illusion of having become good at English
- Students don't continue with English conversation lessons over Skype, so provide an arrangement/ranking/community for continuing

If it were a plan to liven up a stereotypical middle school class reunion, it might look like this:

- It gets stereotyped because the same people always show up → somehow call up the people who don't come
- Have everyone share what they've been doing since middle school beforehand and develop interest in each other

- Carry out something continuous among those who attend class reunions
- Make it a fun event with families involved too
- Play/screen songs, dramas, movies, etc. that were trending during middle school
- Email out YouTube videos of songs, dramas, and movies that were trending during middle school several times starting two weeks beforehand, then having brought back everyone's memories, connect them to the plan for the day
- Carry it out at a restaurant right by campus, and as much as possible invoke memories of those days
- To bring back everyone's memories of middle school, gather photos from back then and make a video montage that's impossible to not watch
- Create a class homepage onto which everyone can upload photos and whatnot from back then

Keeping the content just the way it occurs to you is fine. Once you begin to write in this way, any amount of ideas will naturally come into being. As you go on to write, ideas that roughly seem to fit will appear. Even with similar ideas, write them on a different piece of paper without appending them to a current page. Once you have written them, it is good to line them all up one time on a large desk.

Look over them, and if new ideas are born, write those down right away. If you take twenty to thirty minutes, writing tens of pages, you will feel that you have more or less exhausted your supply. Taken from within these, give the best idea conditional approval. Don't worry about this or that, for it is merely conditional approval. It's fine to choose based on feeling—*Maybe it's this? Yep, it's this!*

For the idea you have given conditional approval to, write one page on each of the following elements of that proposal: Who are you aiming for (target user, target customer)? What is the aim of the proposal? How will you actualize the proposal? In what timeline can/should it be done? How much will it cost? What kind of team does it need to be worked on with? This will likely take ten to fifteen pages.

The crux is to write "without thinking." Instantaneously record it just as you feel it, just as it comes to mind. There is entirely no need to worry about things like structure, degree of clarity, or having a narrative arc. Without such constraints, one's ideas become manyfold richer. Humanity's innate powers of imagination, invention, and creation get put to good use.

"Without thinking" means to record right away whatever comes to mind, as is, without thinking hard on it. When people excessively try to think and think, it becomes difficult to think swiftly and deeply. They try to say something smooth, but in reality they stiffen up. Thoroughly toss that aside. From one to the next, expel onto notes whatever comes to your mind.

If you are conscious of doing this, you will enter a trance of sorts, or rather a state in which ideas come welling up one after another without fail. When one wells up, quickly record it on paper before it disappears. That's what it's like. Although I say "ideas," they will not be the kind that surprise you. *Ah, let's try this* or *what to do about this*—ideas of this caliber will come steadily welling up.

Do not worry at all about coherence, or storyline, or being logical. Even without worrying, these elements will come about in spades. This is the biggest point. With everything at one's disposal, it avoids the dulling of the mind by efforts to consider composition and implement structure.

Laying them out like a card game

From among the tens of pages you have finished writing

(or expelling) in this way, lay out twenty to thirty pages on a desk. There is entirely no need to worry about whether they are low quality, or about their contents. Rather than writing while worrying, as long as you are able to write out just what you feel, just the way it crosses your mind, then you will be fine.

Divide up and spread out the notes you've written by the table of contents, the goals of the proposal, the target customers/users, the concrete functions of your service/app, promotional ideas, option comparisons, schedule, promotion system, necessary funds, anticipated income and expenditure, and so forth. During this time, a slightly larger desk will be necessary.

In the photo, the left end is the cover page, the next page is the table of contents, the next row is each section mentioned in the table of contents, and the next row features several pages tied to each section—such is the order of alignment. While arranging them, revise to a certain extent a number of pages and organize.

Adding and organizing new ideas as they come

As you examine your arrangement of Letter notes on your desk, if new ideas come welling up, set to writing once again. Absolutely do not worry about composition. If the same subject matter is broken up across two pages, consolidate it into one page. If you feel that you haven't written enough, or that something is missing, add another page at once. Always one page within one minute. When you throw them away as well, since every page only took one minute to write, there is nothing precious about them. If you think to write them again, you'll quickly be able to do so. You are capable of writing any number of pages.

When organizing notes, always keep in mind whether

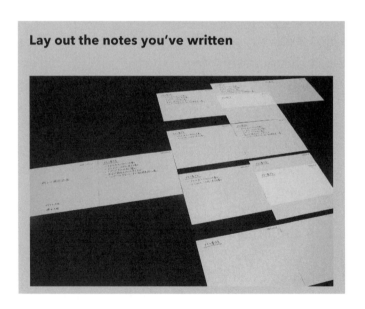

Lay out the notes you've written

or not this proposal will resonate with your target users/customers, whether or not it will move them, and whether or not it will impress them.

To this end, it is necessary from the outset to pinpoint exactly who your target users/customers are. This is surprisingly difficult. There are reasons for this.

The first is assuming things like *who* to target to be self-evident. In reality it is not so self-evident, and it is common to not have a consensus among team members. Even when there is a rough consensus, it's common to still differ over concrete details. In most cases, there is a gap between what one is thinking and what one's team members or partners are thinking. You think it natural that the target users/customers be one group and so do not say so out loud, and consequently only well after the fact does this gap come to light. Even though you were planning on creating a proposal targeting women in their twenties, your team was targeting women starting in their late twenties, focusing on women in their thirties, and also including women in their forties. Or, though you were targeting male *otaku* in their thirties, your team was targeting game-loving men in their late twenties. Such rudimentary mistakes are very much so possible.

The second is not having finished whittling down

one's target. As a target, "women in their twenties" is too broad. Depending on whether it's "urban women in their twenties who live in their parents' home" or "female regular employees in their twenties who live alone and spend 300 dollars or more each month on clothing/cosmetics," the type of proposal which would resonate with each widely differs.

The third is the fundamental problem of not really considering the target users/customers in the first place, or, to say more, of not having the attitude to do so. Such people, for the most part, do not try very hard to produce ideas around the question of *for whom?* They come to halt at thinking *this is somehow interesting*. Steadily producing ideas without worrying about composition and whatnot is an entirely different story from thinking it fine to not consider for whom a proposal would be of interest.

Accordingly, with target users/customers, rather than drafting a rough sketch, determine them as concretely and vividly as possible. It is normal for the target to be considerably different for each idea. For the "Proposal for a new English education in which anyone can become able to speak English" from before, the target users would be broken up into the following:

- High school students especially passionate about studying English
- Hard-working university students who truly wish to master English and have study abroad on their radars
- Working adults in their twenties with high aspirations aiming to study abroad within several years
- Working adults in their thirties set to be stationed abroad in Asia, for whom English has suddenly become necessary
- Working adults in their forties whose parent company abruptly became part of a foreign capital group who are now obliged to give explanations in English to their higher-ups
- English teachers whose interest in English education suddenly swelled, and who are now obliged to demonstrate examples of smooth English conversations

Since the learning environment, needs, and budget of each is completely different, failing to consider them separately is bound to produce what anyone would find to be a flat, nonresonant proposal.

Balancing the whole

Once you've added five or ten more pages, try rearranging them once more. While rearranging them this time around, consider whether your colleagues, superiors, customers, or investors will be pleased or impressed by the content. If it does not fit to a tee, change up the order, write new notes, and adjust accordingly. Try again and again to get into the headspace of your superiors, your customers, your investors, then make modifications as you go.

Revising one place will warrant revisions in other places too. Revising those places will mean more revisions elsewhere. By repeating over and over again the cycle of revising then reexamining the whole, you will be able to explain proposals with an exacting flow.

Once you grow used to note-taking, reaching this point can be done within thirty minutes to an hour's time. In short, this is the process of releasing the contents of your mind in one sitting, examining them and again writing in fresh realizations at the same time, and molding them into place while making modifications at hyperspeed.

Writing in PowerPoint while referencing notes

Once you have the skeleton of your proposal in place, PowerPoint (or Keynote) comes into play for the first time. While referencing the notes you've lined up on your desk, go on to create the cover page, table of contents page, and pages for each section. Some pages may have only titles, other pages only three to four lines, but this is no issue. Reproduce your notes exactly as is.

During this period as well, rather than as a stage for consideration, think of this as a time to rapidly input information into PowerPoint while referencing your notes. Create and single-mindedly fill in the corresponding pages. After booting up PowerPoint, the pace is to input everything you've written within thirty minutes or so and complete the overall composition.

At this point in time, everything you have written on notes, everything you have jotted down, will have been imported into PowerPoint. In this connection, you can staple your original notes and save them as a record, but there is no longer any need to reread them. This is because they're all in your mind now, and their PowerPoint versions are improved and far easier to read.

What comes after is the work of filling out each page while reviewing the table of contents and pages for each section. Regarding the ideas you input directly from handwritten notes, ideas about how to refine them will come steadily welling up. Go on to apply those as much as possible.

Having reached this point, it will be extraordinarily easy to make progress, and your proposal writing will proceed without stress. By individually adjusting each idea without worrying too much about the overall composition, the details with steadily fall into place.

Allowing your proposal several days to ripen then raising it to the next level with meticulous revisions

Having once finished up your proposal, leave it alone for at least one day. If possible, several days is even better. Since the proposal is tentatively finished up, and since there are no more missing pages that need to be finished by the due date, temporarily do something else.

Done in this way, without feeling any pressure, to a certain extent you will be able to take on an objective point of view. At that time, many realizations about the opaqueness of certain areas, or about ways to improve it, will materialize. Make these amendments bit by bit. Then leave it alone once again. Giving your proposal this time to ripen will boost the quality by an astonishing degree.

The way of doing this at McKinsey is more aggressive—namely, to think exhaustively and complete the project's written report and written proposal up until roughly one week before presenting to the client. They also do things like thereupon destroying and reconstructing those documents. This is to temporarily destroy them after having reached the level of being able to sufficiently report to the client. Although I say *destroy*, because the necessary analysis and plans of action are finished, in a mere matter of several hours it is possible to shuffle around the narrative components and reorganize the ways of grasping and viewing the points at issue.

This is based on the notion that the steps to problem-solving and the most effective ways to communicate with clients are not always consistent. In most cases, through this work, a written report which can far and away more effectively appeal to the client is born in the previous one's place.

Note-taking and your team members, family

Having them write notes

With note-taking, you can expect larger results if undertaken with all of one's team members, rather than just practicing it by oneself. First off, your team's overall pace will improve. Since everyone will be aiming for each page within one minute, the speed of all considerations, analyses, decisions, and implementations will rise. The tendency of most people to fall into the trap of thinking in circles will greatly diminish. Endless arguments over responsibilities and the division of roles will practically disappear.

Best of all, as you will develop a common language, you will be able to swiftly reach mutual understandings, thus eliminating discord, and so you will be able to further projects extraordinarily efficiently.

If everyone is practicing note-taking, even in times when friction seems to be arising within the team, each member will write notes on it, so it will be prevented before it takes hold. Even if friction does arise, it can be resolved promptly. In other words, your team's self-regeneration function will be reinforced, and its ability to unite strengthened.

To my delight and surprise, I have been asked before whether it is fine to teach note-taking to children. A father had begun note-taking and, upon learning this, his elementary schooler and wife began as well. Even elementary school students are sufficiently capable of note-taking, and if they start training from that age, their future will be very bright.

Writing notes while listening to their worries

The note-taking I've explained thus far has all been something to write by oneself. The truth is, if you listen to others while writing what they tell you into note format, it is common to receive elated feedback that doing so helped them organize their minds or relieve themselves of what had been bothering them. This is because many people are in trouble because they are unable to sort out their feelings.

If you continue with note-taking for a month, writing 300 pages, your task organization skills will improve so much that it won't be too much to say that you're a completely different person. You will become able to skillfully sort out what others tell you for them.

In this scenario, the format is to record in writing the main points of what is being told to you, so there is no particular need to rush time-wise. While lending your ear to the stories of whoever is confused or distraught, you will write down the main points for them one at a time.

By writing out notes for others, their negative emotions and victim mentality will be alleviated to an extent, and you can have them feeling readier to move forward.

Pass on to your partner the notes you've written. Done in this way, since most will have an interest in note-taking, it is good to briefly instruct them in its methods and, if possible, have them write several pages then and there. This does not mean 100% of their feelings will fit into those pages, so if you suggest they write ten to twenty more pages after returning home, you can likely have them better sense the effects of their notes. For having suggested notes, your reputation, too, will remarkably improve.

Chapter 5

Organizing
and
Utilizing Notes

Organizing notes in clear folders

When writing notes every day, you will amass quite an amount. Though even just writing out any feelings of unease will have a thoroughly large effect, if you skillfully organize them into clear folders, you will become even more mentally organized. The most effective method is to use clear folders.

Writing ten pages of notes every day amounts to 140 pages in two weeks. Since leaving these as is will make them impossible to organize later on, I recommend sorting them into five to ten categories after four or five days have passed since beginning note-taking. Concretely

Stick labels on clear folders

speaking, prepare Letter-size clear folders, stick labels on them, then organize (see photo).

While considering the length of the folder's name, affix a label roughly three centimeters from the bottom. This spacing is due to the fact that once a folder's contents become thicker, labels placed too close to the bottom will peel off.

For folder names, writing with a Magic Marker instead of a ballpoint pen or otherwise makes them easier to see. For this purpose alone, I keep one Magic Marker in both my home and at my work office.

Write folder names in Magic Marker

New Idea

Categories are easy to do if you divide them according to your fields of interest or fields in which you frequently practice note-taking. In my case, I divide them in the following way (in addition to these, I have a special folder for each project):

1. Visions for the Future/Things I Want to Do
2. Communicating with Others
3. Team Management
4. New Ideas
5. Thoughts
6. Information Gathering
7. Stories I've Heard
8. Meetings

1. In "Visions for the Future/Things I Want to Do," I put notes I've written that relate to things I'm thinking of doing thereafter, things I think I want to do, ways I've thought of to break out of whatever present situation I'm in, and so on. It's not frequent, but this is where I put notes with content that will become my heart's compass.

2. "Communicating with Others" is the topic I worry about the most. I have always thought about how

to most effectively communicate with coworkers or people from other companies. My biggest interest is in how to take a strong interest in what someone is saying and hit it off with them right away. There are times when I can do this well, but there are also times when as soon as a meeting starts, I feel that try as I might, I cannot communicate well with some person, and ruminate on how to quickly bring the meeting to an end. After such meetings, I have always written many notes. What I can do to deal with people more cheerfully is also an important theme for me.

3. "Team Management" became a crucial theme for me quickly after I started at McKinsey. In a situation where I had little experience as a consultant, it was necessary for me to skillfully mobilize four to six client team members to perform a vast amount of analysis and interviewing, and to give suggestions that would drastically improve the company's results. From my fourth year, since I was grappling with management innovation for LG Group, it was necessary to simultaneously orchestrate ten or more different projects, and to create an environment in which each McKinsey member and client team member could

steadily produce results. Also within the start-up co-founding and management support in which I'm principally involved in now, elevating the productivity of projects and start-up teams—or "creating a winning team"—is a perpetual challenge. Accordingly, I consider a lot. Think of a lot. And, there are many times when I reflect on how I could have done something better.

4. "New Ideas" is, just as it sounds, for new ideas about business or how to do something well. I quickly write whenever something occurs to me, or when something inspires me. *Why didn't I think of that? What could I have done to think of that?* —I steadily write thoughts like this down as well.

   While there is a gap between people who execute ideas they've hit upon and those who, upon hearing that, regretfully think *I was just thinking that* or *I could have thought of that if only I had done this*, without worrying about it, write it down into notes. In saying that, perhaps it would be more accurate to call it "This and That Related to New Ideas."

5. "Thoughts" is for the frequent thoughts and concerns which do not fall into any of the aforemen-

tioned categories. I write on a broad range of things, such as how to produce better results at work, or what needs to be done for Japanese people to become able to speak English.

6. In the "Information Gathering" folder, I've written notes on ways to gather information, ways to sort it efficiently, ways to search and retrieve material I've gathered, on what worked well and what did not, and so on. I put in all notes relating to thoughts or concerns about information gathering. While there are many people who are not particular about information gathering, it is in fact extremely important for making one's mind flexible, and also for cultivating a wide variety of applicable knowledge.

How one efficiently gathers information in a small amount of time each day, how one increases their expertise daily, and how they use it—these have a big effect on one's growth when examined in units of several months. So, I've always deliberately written notes related to information gathering.

In this field, new services that increase productivity are released one after another, and because each time it is necessary to slightly modify one's methodology, it is wasteful to relax one's vigilance.

This is because by the time you notice, a far better method is already gaining popularity.

7. "Stories I've Heard" do not, to tell the truth, fall into the note-taking which I've described in this book. When I hear an amazing story at dinner gatherings or lectures, I without fail take thorough notes on Letter paper. These are the same as what society normally thinks of notes to be, and I try to as much as possible record these stories word for word without omitting anything. As such, in this case alone, on Letter paper, rather than four to six lines, I write tightly packed from top to bottom.

Concretely speaking, on horizontal pieces of Letter paper, I write from top to bottom on the left half of the pages, then when I reach the bottom I continue writing in the same way from the top of the right half. The content is dense, so I continue writing at a staggering speed. In the case of an hour-long lecture, this turns into roughly three to five pages. I make a point of being certain to record down the important points.

At dinner gatherings and the like, I have times when I feel afraid of what others may think of my taking notes. These are situations when taking notes would put someone on guard and stop their conversation, or when by no means does taking notes seem feasible atmosphere-wise. At such times I, on the train home, write five to seven pages, recreating the scene in my mind. Across doing this time after time, I became able to recreate in notes important stories I'd heard while mostly not leaving anything out. With dinner gatherings, due to the fact that exceeding two hours is normal, this becomes a considerable amount to remember.

However, as I have times when just numbers grow fuzzy in my memory, I try to take notes in the bathroom part way through. This is because, as one would expect, recording numbers in writing right in front of someone is bound to stop their story in its tracks.

In this regard, my "Stories I've Heard" folder is becoming a treasury of wisdom. While it might be a slightly surprising way of splitting things up, it is quite a convenient method. It's not limited to this, but any time you are classifying something, creating an "Other" file will result in less puzzlement. Although "Stories I've Heard" is not an "Other" file, it allows me to add in that breadth of versatility.

8. The notes which I put in the "Meetings" folder are written in the same way as the notes in "Stories I've Heard." Every day, I attend a number of meetings and conferences and quickly record in writing anything necessary to document. In cases where there are many notes and materials for a project, I organize those in their own folder, but the more self-contained ones get filed away here.

   In this connection, there are also situations when Legal-size or Ledger-size materials are distributed at meetings. In that case, I fold them in half with the content facing outwards, then file them away into the relevant folders.

Re-examining folder categories

With folder categories, it is fine for you to either follow my aforementioned recommendations or to tweak them to your liking. Around the time you surpass one hundred pages of notes, it's possible to feel that your folder divisions don't quite fit right depending on your awareness of issues, your circumstances, or your needs. A signal of this would be if several notes of which you are unsure which folder to use surface when filing away your notes before bed each night.

For example:

1. Supposing you've created folders titled "Team Leadership" and "Team Management,"
2. And over and over you find yourself unsure of which one to put notes you've written into,
3. And supposing titles related to "leadership" always come to mind, and you've written a large volume of corresponding notes:

Combine the two folders "Team Leadership" and "Team Management" into a single folder titled "Leadership." Take out all of the notes filed in the original two folders, reorganize them by date, and throw them into the new folder. In other words, "Team Leadership" and "Team Management" were keywords for you, and you planned to sort using them, but in your mind they were not all that clearly separated.

If that day forward as you continue to write more notes you become able to throw them into the "Leadership" folder without hesitating, then your new folder divisions were correct.

There are also times to separate one folder into two. If the notes you place in your "Team Management" folder are broadly divided into subordinate management and project team management, and if you continue feeling every time you go to file one away that one is subordinate management or that another is project management, then it is best to separate that folder into two.

There are also times when although your folder divisions do not leave you perplexed, the folder names may not fit well.

In that case, rewrite them without delay. For example, even if a folder began titled as "Leadership," if most of the notes are regarding CEO leadership, expressing it as "CEO Leadership" will fit more closely. I try to make changes any time I think this might be the case.

Regarding the category "Communicating with Others," if your notes relating to ways of dealing with people, or to relationship building, increase by a few and look to continue increasing, then you can reconsider slightly and change the name to "Communicating and Dealing with Others."

To this end, I do a decent amount of scheming over folder labels. This is because since it is necessary to modify folder names several times over, I want the labels I use to be easy to stick on and hard-pressed to come unstuck, yet easily removable when it becomes necessary to do so. As far as I know, there is one type of label which fulfills the requirements of these conflicting purposes: Post-it's Labeling & Cover-up Tape. I draw out approximately enough to fit my folder title, tear it off, and stick it on. And I'm always sure to write new titles in Magic Marker.

This minor work is in fact considerably tied in with my mental organization. There are supposedly people who feel more at ease when their desk is in disarray, but as for

me I prefer to organize whatever can be organized (and as a result I spend almost no time looking for things; my materials ordinarily surface within a few seconds). The key is the same as with folders. It is the method of sorting into several precise categories, revising those categories until they fit perfectly, and afterwards creating a place to put the miscellaneous leftovers.

With folder categories, after settling on them once via this method, the need to modify them will go away. Your awareness of the issues will be set in order, and you will have the sensation that the notes you write fit precisely into the right folders. At times that you change jobs, are promoted, or change roles, there will be a need to reconsider slightly, but having your folder divisions organized once, you will become able to relatively easily revise your folder categories. It is also possible to say that by carrying out the organization of your mind using folders right before your eyes, you will establish the know-how and steps for making category revisions.

When you begin new work or involvements, create new folders. In my case, these would be "Clean Tech," "3D Printer," and so on. Both of these I created when I began a new activity. It's quite refreshing work.

Notes thereafter

I stack my clear folders on the left side of my desk. Every night before bed, just by throwing the ten pages written that day into whichever folders, it is possible to organize them in a moment's time.

Once folders grow thick, I stick a number on them and store such old folders separately. The pile on the left side of my desk is roughly five to seven centimeters thick. Any more than that and they become difficult to handle. There is a selection of clear folders which I sometimes carry

Roughly how many note folders I keep stacked on my desk

around with me, but the majority get left on my desk.

What I must be careful of is that they are not seen by other people. On these notes, I purge my dissatisfactions, awareness of issues, *everything*. People's names also appear. In cases where there is a possibility they might be seen by company employees or family members, properly storing them away provides more peace of mind.

How to store notes

Writing ten pages every day will amount to 1800 pages in six months, 3600 pages in a year. It is best to hold

Several years' worth of the author's folders

onto these, by no means throwing them away. They become proof of one's growth. As I will explain later, once six months have passed since writing a note, there will no longer be any need to revisit it. However, the notes' existence itself is proof of the accumulation of one's thoughts and is bound to become a source of confidence.

Since 300 or so pages fit into one clear folder, 3600 pages would mean twelve clear folders' worth. Stacked up, they do not take up a significant amount of space. I store all of my past notes in cardboard boxes. Placed on top of a bookshelf, they do not become much of a nuisance either. Space might also be a problem for some, but as much as possible, this is the method I'd like to recommend.

Generally, do not look back on notes

In your clear folders, add the notes you write each day to the top. Ordinarily, there is absolutely no need to review them. Throw them in once you write them—that's it. If a similar title occurs to you, then write it again. Write again without hesitating. It's only one minute, and it is best to expel the contents of your mind.

As I have already mentioned, rather than reviewing what you have written previously, it is best to freshly rewrite. Titles and main text will somewhat differ, but this does not matter in the slightest. Since it is not the case that you will be comparing them to begin with, it is no problem at all if they are a tad different. Writing over and over on themes and titles that you are hung up on will become, frankly, supremely important practice. Each time, your feelings of unease will be translated into language and expressed, and by confirming them with your eyes, their transformation into words will deepen even more.

With themes and topics you are hung up on, it is possible to write on them from five or six to ten times or more across several weeks to several months, but in writing that much you will completely grasp their contents, and you will arrive at a state of having a huge weight lifted off your shoulders. Your mind will be perfectly organized.

When I initially started at McKinsey, I wrote and wrote over and over again on themes like "How to do interviews?" "How to summarize the outcome of an interview?" "How to do client team management?" and "For finalizing written reports?"

Through this, I grasped the optimal measures to take and rapidly honed my skills while confirming each skill fundamental to consulting.

Organizing your folders
and taking a brief look every three months

Within each category in the clear folders you've thrown notes into, it is fine to simply stash them away. This is because by spewing out, or rather sweeping out, all of the anxieties that come to your mind, you will already be securing satisfactory effects. Even without revisiting each one, by continuing to write anew as you go, your mind will sharply improve; the wheels will begin turning.

However, in order to also confirm your growth process, it is good to take a brief look once every three months. Newer notes will be at the top of your folders, so for each folder arrange them in reverse order with the oldest note on top, rearranged by date. This can be done in a few minutes. With that done, take just a few minutes to skim through them. That will be enough.

Organize all of your folders in the same way and take a brief look. At ten pages every day, writing for three months will amount to 900 pages, the sight of which provides a tremendous sense of accomplishment. And you are bound to make many discoveries as well, thinking *huh? I was thinking about something like that back then—I guess I was worried about things like this.*

Even at a pace of three to four pages every day, or

roughly 300 pages in three months, there will be many discoveries. I want for you to resolve from that day forward to write ten pages each day while reflecting on the past.

Re-examining once more after another three months

After another three months (six months after writing notes), again organize the notes that have been added since, and just one more time re-examine the portion you reread last time. Having done this, you will be surprised that the majority are securely in your mind.

With some notes, the content will be so persuasive and coherent that you will wonder who was able to write so well. Who? Well, you, of course.

By rereading them after three months and again after six months, you will know what you were worried about, what you decided to do about it, and how it unfolded thereafter. You will be able to trace back the path you have taken. Going beyond that will be mostly unnecessary. In other words, as a general rule, there is no need to reread your notes after you have revisited them twice, once after three months and once after six months. There is a large merit to when you first write them, and two rereads will allow you to digest them—this will already be enough.

CHAPTER 5: Organizing and Utilizing Notes

In Conclusion

Beginning with the question of why people are unable to think deeply, up until this point I have remarked on the truly useful mental training method which until now has not been spoken of anywhere. Drawn from considerations in the ways in which our innate ability to think is impeded and what can be done to retrieve it, this is the method which I myself, having written tens of thousands of pages, have taught to around one thousand people.

For the vast majority of people, attempting to assemble one's thoughts brings their mind to a halt. I've explained that by clearing whatever out onto notes just the way you felt it, without trying to finalize, and without trying to think, your thinking will progress as much as you'd like.

The ultimate result is "Zero Second Thinking." The feeling that you are not good at thinking will disappear, and regarding situation assessment, task organization, and

real-life behaviors, ideas will quickly come to you. If you continue ten-pages-a-day note-taking for several months, I believe you will gradually come to know the sensation of "Zero Second Thinking."

In 2012, when I facilitated business planning workshops for manufacturing industry leaders in Mumbai and Kolkata, I introduced "note-taking" to them as well, and had them each write ten pages.

The photo is of a workshop in Mumbai—it was quite the spectacle to see 120 management leaders from midsize and large companies in the manufacturing industry simultaneously performing note-taking. Everyone had a strong desire to grow, and I was moved by their sincere attitude towards work (to the effect that I had them appreciate the spirit of Japan's manufacturing industry, the training room became a place to take off one's shoes, and this was the scene).

From here on out as well, even if done alone, I would be honored to have many people undertake note-taking with the goal of achieving "Zero Second Thinking," to have them use their refreshed minds to bring a sharpness to their work, and to have them lead fulfilled private lives, too.

Lastly, I would be happy to hear your impressions of this book at akaba@b-t-partners.com.

I will get back to you right away. Also, if you send images or PDFs of notes you have written, I will give feedback on formatting and the like.

Author
Yuji Akaba

After graduating from Tokyo University's Department of Engineering in 1978, Yuji Akaba was engaged at Komatsu Ltd. in the planning and development of dump trucks for use at construction sites. From 1983, he completed a Master of Science and an Engineer Degree, both in Mechanical Engineering, at Stanford University. In 1986, he entered McKinsey. There, he led numerous projects in management strategy planning and execution support, organizational planning and introduction, marketing, launching new enterprises, and so on. In 1990, while launching McKinsey's Seoul office from the ground up and serving as the driving force in its ascent to more than 120 employees, he gave support to Korean companies, particularly to LG Group's rapid global progress. In 2002, he co-founded Breakthrough Partners with the mission of helping entrepreneurs start up, develop, and build world-class venture businesses based in Japan. Recently, he is actively engaged in management innovation, developing human resources in management, creating new enterprises, and open innovation for large companies.

website: http://b-t-partners.com/
Blog: http://b-t-partners.com/akaba/
Twitter: https://twitter.com/YujiAkaba

Zero Second Thinking
The world's simplest training for improving your mind

© Yuji Akaba 2019
First Published in Japan with 2013 by DIAMOND, Inc.

ISBN: 978-1-64273-046-3

Written by Yuji Akaba
Translated by Evan Bauer
Edited by Yumi Itabashi
English Edition Published by Yuji Akaba 2019

Printed in Japan
1 2 3 4 5 6 7 8 9 10

http://b-t-partners.com/